Delight

J. B. Priestley was born in Bradford in 1894. He was educated locally and later worked as a junior clerk in a wool office. After serving in the army throughout the First World War he went to Trinity Hall, Cambridge, before setting up in London as a critic and renowned essayist. He won great acclaim and success with his novel *The Good Companions*, 1929. This and his next novel *Angel Pavement*, 1930, earned him an international reputation. Other notable works of fiction include *Bright Day, Lost Empires* and *The Image Men*.

In 1932 he began a new career as a dramatist with *Dangerous Corner*, and went on to write many other well-known plays such as *Time and the Conways, Johnson Over Jordan, Laburnum Grove, An Inspector Calls, When We Are Married, Eden End, The Linden Tree* and *A Severed Head* which he wrote with Iris Murdoch. His plays have been translated and performed all over the world and many have been filmed. *An Inspector Calls* is still taught on the GCSE English Literature curriculum.

In the 1930s Priestley became increasingly concerned about social justice. *English Journey*, published in 1934, was a seminal account of his travels through England. During the Second World War his regular Sunday night radio *Postscripts* attracted audiences of up to 14 million. Priestley shored up confidence and presented a vision of a better world to come.

In 1958 he became a founder member of the Campaign for Nuclear Disarmament and later in life represented the UK at two UNESCO conferences.

Among his other important books are *Literature and Western Man*, a survey of Western literature over the past 500 years, his memoir *Margin Released*, and *Journey Down a Rainbow* which he wrote with his third wife, the archaeologist Jacquetta Hawkes. J. B. Priestley refused both a knighthood and a peerage but accepted the Order of Merit in 1977. He died in 1984. His ashes were buried near Hubberholme Church in the Yorkshire Dales.

J. B. Priestley

Delight

Look thy last on all things lovely,
Every hour. Let no night
Seal thy sense in deathly slumber
Till to delight
Thou have paid thy utmost blessing ...

Walter de la Mare

Harper
North

HarperNorth
Windmill Green
Mount Street
Manchester, M2 3NX

A division of
HarperCollins*Publishers*
1 London Bridge Street
London SE1 9GF

www.harpercollins.co.uk

HarperCollins*Publishers*
Macken House, 39/40 Mayor Street Upper
Dublin1, D01 C9W8, Ireland

First published by William Heinemann Ltd 1949
This edition published by HarperNorth in 2023

1 3 5 7 9 10 8 6 4 2

For the family
These small amends
With the old monster's love

Contents

Contents

Contents

Preface

or the Grumbler's Apology

I have always been a grumbler. All the records, going back to earliest childhood, establish this fact. Probably I arrived here a malcontent, convinced that I had been sent to the wrong planet. (And I feel even now there is something in this.) I was designed for the part, for I have a sagging face, a weighty underlip, what I am told is "a saurian eye", and a rumbling but resonant voice from which it is difficult to escape. Money could not buy a better grumbling outfit.

In the West Riding of Yorkshire, where I spent my first nineteen years, all local customs and prejudices favour the grumbler. To a good West Riding type there is something shameful about praise, that soft Southern trick. But fault-finding and blame are constant and hearty. The edge of criticism up there is sharpened every morning. So the twilight of Victoria and the brief but golden afternoon of Edward the Seventh discovered Jackie Priestley grumbling away, a novice of course but learning fast. A short spell of the Wool Trade – and in no trade do you hear more complaints and bitter murmurs – developed my technique. Then came the First World War, in which I served with some of the dourest unwearying grumblers that even the British Army has ever known, and was considered to hold my own with the best of them. After that, a rapidly ripening specimen, I grumbled my way through Cambridge, Fleet Street, and various fields of literary and dramatic enterprise. I have grumbled all over the world, across seas, on mountains, in deserts. I have grumbled as much at home as abroad, and so I have been the despair of my womenfolk.

Not that they ever understood what I was up to. We have always been at cross-purposes here. The feminine view appears to be that grumbling only makes things worse, whereas I have always held that a fine grumble makes things better. If, for example, an hotel gives me a bad breakfast, I have only to grumble away for a few minutes to feel that some reasonable balance has been restored: the grumble has been subtracted from the badness of the breakfast. So it is no use crying to me "Oh – do be quiet! It's bad enough without your grumbling." My mind does not move along these lines. If I have not had a good breakfast, I argue, at least I have had a good grumble. Thus I have always been innocent of the major charge – that of trying deliberately to make things worse.

Another point for the defence is that I have always looked and sounded much worse than I felt. When I am displeased – but not when I am pleased, I gather – for some reason, still hidden from me, I tend to overact my part. Often when I am feeling merely annoyed, a little put out, I appear to be blazingly angry or lost in the deepest sulks. The appearance is larger than the reality. And I have suffered much from this suggestion of the theatre or the public platform in my private behaviour. Time and again my real feelings have been misinterpreted. I may not have been enjoying myself, but at least I have not been suffering as intensely as the rest of the company imagined. (When rehearsals are going badly, I am often rushed out of the theatre, given drinks, flattered, cajoled, simply to keep me out of sight of the players, those pampered creatures.) Once, years ago, at a large party, when I was grumbling as usual, a young woman who was a stranger to me turned on me fiercely and told me I had better go home instead of trying to spoil other people's pleasure. I was taken aback, and may be said to have stayed aback ever since. But though I would gladly send that woman an inscribed copy of this book – and regret I do not know her name, and hope all is well with her – the fact remains that she was misjudging me. The growling she overheard – for, dash it, I wasn't talking to her – was a kind of small talk, almost a social gesture. My discontent was not meant to be taken seriously. It was that old unconscious exaggeration again. And although perhaps I always ought to have been more careful, for this I am more to be pitied than to be blamed.

A final point for the defence. Much of my writing, I have no doubt, consists of adverse criticism of this life, and so is a sort of grumbling at large. There is some self-indulgence here, I will grant you, but there is also a speck or two of something better. For I have always felt that a writer, if only to justify some of his privileges, should speak for those who cannot easily speak for themselves. He may run into trouble – and I have gone headlong into whole cliffsides of it – but at least nobody is going to give him the sack, leave him with a mortgage and four children who need shoes, if he comes out and tells the truth. I have therefore often grumbled in print more on other people's behalf than on my own. Again, I am always led instinctively into opposition to the party in power and to all persons dressed in authority. I am a toady in reverse. I would not describe myself as a born rebel, for I have no fanaticism, but there is in me a streak of the jeering anarchist, who parts company even with his friends when they have succeeded to power. Moreover, having been fortunate in many respects, I have felt a dislike of appearing too conscious of good fortune, and some of my fault-finding and complaining has been a determined avoidance of *hubris*, like so much "touching wood". And of course this has meant more grumbling.

So many a decent fellow, showing a better face to his bad luck than ever I appear to have shown to my good luck, must have cried in his exasperation: "Does this chap never enjoy anything?" And my reply, long overdue, is this book. And nobody can complain that I have waited until everything in the garden was lovely. The present state of the world – but no, we know about that. We can also bolt the door of the madhouse of our economic life, public and private, ignoring for once the mopping and mowing throng of bank managers, accountants, tax collectors. But during the period when I was trying to sort out, capture, record these memories and impressions of delight, I have had the nastiest flop I have ever had in the Theatre, we have coped with two weddings, sundry illnesses, and the longest and noisiest moving-house I ever remember, and I have had most of my remaining teeth pulled out, two at a time at intervals nicely calculated to keep every nerve in my head jangling, together with a minor sentence of forced fasting and reluctant self-mortification. In fact, most of the anxieties and miseries of an author, a parent, a householder, and an ageing sedentary male have been thrust upon me; and the life of Reilly, which some people imagine me to lead, has been further away than a fading dream. Nevertheless, through the prevailing thick and the occasional thin, I have kept close to this little book on *Delight*, so that it could be my apology, my bit of penitence, for having grumbled so much, for having darkened the breakfast table, almost ruined the lunch, nearly silenced the dinner party, for all the fretting and chafing, grousing and croaking, for the old glum look and the thrust-out lower lip. So, my long-suffering kinsfolk, my patient friends, may a glimmer of that delight which has so often possessed me, but perhaps too frequently in secret, now reach you from these pages.

1

Fountains

Fountains. I doubt if I ever saw one, even the smallest, without some tingling of delight. They enchant me in the daytime, when the sunlight ennobles their jets and sprays and turns their scattered drops into diamonds. They enchant me after dark when coloured lights are played on them, and the night rains emeralds, rubies, sapphires. And, best of all, when the last colour is whisked away, and there they are in a dazzling white glory! The richest memory I have of the Bradford Exhibition of my boyhood, better than even the waterchute or the Somali Village or the fireworks, is of the Fairy Fountain, which changed colour to the waltzes of the Blue Hungarian Band, and was straight out of the Arabian Nights. And I believe my delight in these magical jets of water, the invention of which does credit to our whole species, is shared by ninety-nine persons out of every hundred. But where are they, these fountains we love? We hunger for them and are not fed. A definite issue could be made out of this, beginning with letters to the *Times*, continuing with meetings and unanimous resolutions and deputations to Downing Street, and ending if necessary with processions and mass demonstrations and some rather ugly scenes. What is the use of our being told that we live in a democracy if we want fountains and have no fountains? Expensive? Their cost is trifling compared to that of so many idiotic things we are given and do not want. Our towns are crammed with all manner of rubbish that no people in their senses ever asked for, yet where are the fountains? By all means let us have a policy of full employment, increased production, no gap between exports and imports, social security, a balanced This and a planned That, but let us also have fountains – more and more fountains – higher and higher fountains – fountains like wine, like blue and green fire, fountains like diamonds – and rainbows in every square. Crazy? Probably. But with hot wars and cold wars we have already tried going drearily mad. Why not try going delightfully mad? Why not stop spouting ourselves and let it be done for us by graceful fountains, exquisite fountains, beautiful fountains?

2

Shopping in small places

Shopping in small towns and villages. When I am in cities and surrounded by shops I take no pleasure in buying things and generally contrive to have my shopping done for me. Take me away from shops, however, and then after a week or two let me find my way to some small town or village and I take a delight in buying almost anything. I am as bad as any woman. I am like a sailor after a long voyage. I acquire gadgets and for a day or two have an almost painful loyalty toward them, the gadget and I being like an engaged couple and any criticism being instantly resented. Out of some general store I bring pencils I don't need, dubious scented tobacco, boiled sweets I have to give away, horrible stationery, travel books by Victorian clergymen, balls of string, patent medicines, hairy little note-books, boxes of paper fasteners. There is practically nothing I cannot be sold if

J. B. Priestley

I have been long enough away from shops. The truth is – and statesmen should take note of the fact – that spending money in shops has gone on so long among us that it is now an instinctive activity. Drawing free rations is not a substitute for it, which is something Communist governments often fail to understand. We have now developed deep unconscious urges to shop. We begin as small children clutching our pennies and staring over the counter in a sweet agony of indecision. After being away from shops or not having the money to spend, our delight arises from the knowledge that notes and coins can be exchanged for more fascinating objects and from the feeling of having a wide delicious choice. It is here that the old-fashioned village shop is superior to the most grandiose city store just because it offers the widest possible choice in the smallest possible area: the hungry eye is at once offered a feast. We who begin to buy only when we are at the mercy of our instinctive drives do not want a whole floor of neckties or saucepans, with lifts to take us to cushions or tobacco. It is when shaving brushes and cheese, toffee and potato peelers, liver pills and socks, are heaped together that we go berserk, shopping like mad.

3

Detective stories in bed

Reading detective stories in bed. I find this delightful at home, and even more delightful when I am away from home, a lost man. The fuss of the day is done with; you are snugly installed in bed, in a little lighted place of your own; and now to make the mind as cosy as the body! But why detective stories? Why not some good literature? Because, with a few happy exceptions – and there are far too few of them – good literature, which challenges and excites the mind, will not do. In my view, it should be read away from the bedroom. But why not some dull solemn stuff, portentous memoirs, faded works of travel, soporifics bound in calf? Here I can speak only for myself. But if my bed book is too dull then I begin to think about my own work and then sleep is banished for hours. No, the detective story is the thing, and its own peculiar virtues have not been sufficiently appreciated. The worst attempt

I ever heard the *Brains Trust* make was at a question concerning the popularity of detective stories. The wise men waffled on about violence and crime, missing the point by miles. (But then a man who enjoyed his detective stories at night would not bother being on the *Brains Trust*.) We enthusiasts are not fascinated by violence or the crime element in these narratives. Often, like myself, we deplore the blood-and-bones atmosphere and wish the detective novelists were not so conventional about offering us murder all the time. (A superb detective story could be written – and I have half a mind to write it – about people who were not involved in any form of crime. About disappearance or a double life, for example.) Please remember that most serious fiction now has ceased to appeal to our taste for narrative. The novelist may be a social critic, a philosopher, a poet, or a madman, but he is no longer primarily a story-teller. And there are times when we do not want anybody's social criticism or deep psychological insight or prose poetry or vision of the world: we want a narrative, an artfully contrived tale. But not any kind of tale, no fragrant romances and the like. What we want – or at least what *I* want, late at night; you can please yourself – is a tale that is in its own way a picture of life but yet has an entertaining puzzle element in it. And this the detective story offers me. It is of course highly conventional and stylised – think of all those final meetings in the library, or those little dinners in Soho (with about six pounds worth of wine) paid for out of a Scotland Yard salary – but its limitations are part of its charm. It opposes to the vast mournful muddle of the real world its own tidy problem and neat solution. As thoughtful citizens we are hemmed in now by gigantic problems that appear as insoluble as they are menacing, so how pleasant it is to take an hour or two off to consider only the problem of the body that locked itself in its study and then used the telephone. *(We know now that Sir Rufus must have died not later than ten o'clock, and yet we know too that he apparently telephoned to Lady Bridget at ten-forty-five – eh, Travers?)* This is easy and sensible compared with the problem of remaining a sane citizen in the middle of the twentieth century. After the newspaper headlines, it is refreshing to enter this well-ordered microcosm, like finding one's way into a garden after wandering for days in a jungle. I like to approach sleep by way of these neat simplifications, most of them as soundly ethical as Socrates himself. It is true that I may burn my bedlight too long, just because I must know how the dead Sir Robert managed to telephone; yet, one problem having been settled for me, I feel I sleep all the sounder for this hour or two's indulgence. And what a delight it is to switch off the day's long chaos, stretch legs that have begun to ache a little, turn on the right side, and then once more find the eccentric private detective moodily playing his violin or tending his orchids, or discover again the grumpy inspector doodling in his office, and know that a still more astonishing puzzle is on its way to him and to me!

4

After finishing some work

After finishing a piece of work that has been long and rather difficult, I have a sense of satisfaction that can expand into delight. This does not come from surveying the work done, for at these times I am rarely sure of the value of what I have just created, am more than doubtful if my first intention has been fulfilled, and may even wonder gloomily, while I hold the work in mind, if I have not been wasting time and energy. No, the delight springs from a sense of release. I have been in prison with this one idea, and now, I feel, I am free. Tomorrow, ten times the size of last Tuesday, is suddenly rich with promise. Time and space are both extended. I catch a glimpse of fifty new ideas, flickering like lizards among the masonry of my mind; but I need not bother about them. I am now the master and not the slave. I can go to China, learn the clarinet, read Gibbon again, study metaphysics, grow strange flowers in hothouses, lie in bed, lunch and dine with old friends and brilliant acquaintances, look at pictures, take the children to concerts, tidy up the study, talk properly to my wife. What a world this is to be free and curious in! What a wealth of sunlight and starlight and firelight! And so for a little while, before the key grates in the lock again, there I am, out and free, with mountains of treasure before my dazzled eyes. Yes, there comes a moment – just a moment – of delight.

5

Meeting a friend

There are some places and situations that offer you nothing but despair. Somehow you cannot be yourself in them. Everybody and everything there cancels you out. You are alone among the Enemy. Anything you say or do or can even imagine yourself saying or doing would mean nothing. You seem to have wandered out of your world, have perhaps lost it for ever. To cope with such situations, such places, such blank-faced monsters, you would have to be born again. You are being asked to exist in strange dimensions. All waking hours begin to seem like a nightmare, and only as the day ends and you retreat thankfully to bed do you catch a gleam of sanity. So what a wonderful thing it is to come unexpectedly in such a place or situation upon a friend! Suddenly – there is the familiar face, with every feature a land-mark in a sensible country. Here are the eyes that see you as your old established self. The strange dimensions have vanished. Into these ears you can pour your talk and be understood. The very sight of that nose restores you to a comprehensible world. "Hel-*lo*! What on earth are *you* doing here?" It is the voice – at last – of an affectionate fellow creature. What delight!

6

Decks in early morning

There is a moment I have been missing for ten years, ever since the war first cut me off from leisurely sea travel. It is the moment of reaching the deck, fairly early in the morning, before breakfast, in fair weather. You come out of sleep, out of the stuffiness below, into all the freshness in the world. During the night everything has been re-made for you. The open parts of the ship, the sea itself, even the morning, have just come back from the laundry. The scrubbed planks glisten and the brasses blaze in a new morning of Creation. The winking and hissing sea has just been invented. The blue above is most delicately pale and as yet untarnished. The air is a mystery of goodness. From these shifting meadows comes the fragrance of invisible sea blossoms. Ocean and air whisper the news of their perfection. It is the morning of Time itself. It is three seconds – while eye and nose and cheek still remember the dark and fug of the night below – of the Golden Age. Merely to breathe is a happy adventure. Nothing can ever seem so clean and fresh again as this empty deck, this vacant tumbling sea, the morning bright from the mint. Ah! – the delight, long-lost and perhaps never to be re-captured, of that turn or two on deck before breakfast.

7

A walking tour

On a dazzling morning in the early summer of 1919 I left
the bus at Buckden, in Upper Wharfedale, to carry my
rucksack over the pass into Wensleydale. I was beginning
a walking tour. But no ordinary one. It was my first since
I had left the army, from which I had recently been demo-
bilised, after enduring four-and-a-half years of what
seemed to me its idiotic routine. I was out of uniform, a
sensible civilian again, careless once and for all as to what
purple-faced grunting military men might think of me. I
had an idle summer before me, after which I would go to
Cambridge. But that was not all. I took with me into the
dales, like an enchanted passport, a commission from the
editor of the *Yorkshire Observer* to write several articles
on my walking tour, to be paid for at the rate of one
guinea per article. It was my first commission of the
kind – though I had done some journalism before the war,
as far back as my middle teens – and I have never had one
since that meant half as much. To write what I pleased

about my walking tour – and to be paid for it – this was tremendous; here was a literary career. Now add up all these items of felicity – the bright morning, Upper Wharfedale, recent demobilisation, the editor's commission – imagine what you would have felt yourself, *then double it*. The track to Aysgarth – for it was still a track then, no motor road – wound up toward the blue; larks sang above the moorland grass; the little streams glittered and gurgled among the rocks; the sun was high, and a wind blew from Paradise. I walked in delight, and now after thirty years I have only to be quiet and to remember, to feel that spring in my heels and my head towering in the golden air. Youth is perhaps an overpraised season, but when all things conspire for it, as they did for me then, it lives fabulously for an hour or two, rocketing into regions afterwards closed to us for ever this side of Heaven. But the articles I wrote were not up to much.

8

Trying new blends of tobacco

Trying new blends of tobacco. I have been smoking steadily ever since 1910 (beginning with Cut Cavendish at 3½d. an ounce); and to this day, if my eye is caught by an unfamiliar package on a tobacconist's shelf, I will try a new blend. I may not smoke it with delight, especially nowadays when good new blends are hard to find and many of the old mixtures are not what they once were, but I enjoy the little adventure. There is a certain pious conservatism in this occasional fickleness toward tried favourites. I am preserving the 1910 spirit in smoking; for in those days tobacco was not sold by young women lost in the myths of Hollywood but by solid middle-aged men, pickled in nicotine themselves, who would pull down their canisters of Old Virginia, Perique or Latakia, mix you something new on the spot if necessary, and lived with you in a community of palates. (It was economy that took me first to Cut Cavendish, for these fellows, if you gave them their head, might run you up to 5d. or even 6d. an ounce.) There were tobacconists in those days. Most of them, with much else of value, seemed to disappear during the First World War, their place being taken by bored pushers of packages across counters. There arrived too a vast new horde of unadventurous and ignorant smokers, mere creatures of habit, born to raise the dividends of tobacco combines and cartels. These robots would start with Somebody's Navy Cut and are puffing away at it to this day, hardly knowing that other tobaccos exist. Notice how in pre-1914 literature – for example, in the entrancing fables of W. W. Jacobs (and what delight *he* has given me!) – sensible fellows toss pouches to each other and say "Try a pipeful of this." And who talks about tobacco now? The country is crowded with men who pay their four-and-something an ounce and yet could not sustain five minutes talk on tobacco. But I go forward, occasionally pointing a finger at a tin or packet I have never noticed before, in the 1910 tradition. And now I must have smoked everything combustible in a pipe, including coltsfoot and various weird herbal mixtures, belonging to the ritual of nature religions rather than to the honest pleasure of smoking. This means of course that I have set fire and puffed away at a good deal of muck. There have been times when decent pipes of mine appear to have been drenched in cheap scent. I remember occasions when you would have thought I had acquired a packet of gunpowder, there was so much sizzling and sparking, so many sulphurous fumes. I have smoked "carefully blended" mixtures that tasted like a hayrick on fire. I have opened tins packed by malevolent wizards, whose spells within half an hour conjured what I took to be tobacco into quarter of a pound of dust. But I regret nothing. I have summoned Europe, America, Africa and Asia to fill my pipe. At my age naturally I have my steady favourites – and, without stopping to advertise, let me say that I like to alternate between an honest Virginia and a full rich mixture, heavy with Latakia – but even now I still follow the gleam. "What's that up there? *Boynton's Benediction*. Well, I'll try it."

9
Gin and tonic, 1940

Just gin and tonic and some potato crisps. But the time and the setting were important. During the *blitz* period, the early autumn of 1940, I was in London, collecting material and writing articles during the day and broadcasting very late at night to the Dominions and America. It was exhausting work and I was always short of sleep. On Friday afternoons I went down to an Oxfordshire village, where my wife was staying for a few weeks, and then returned to London on Sunday afternoon, to give my Postscript talk in the evening. I would arrive at this village on Friday about an hour or so before dinner, after which I crept to bed, to make up for the week's loss of sleep. Nobody wanted me in the house during this hour before dinner, so I used to stroll down the road to the village pub, where I would drink gin and tonic and nibble potato crisps. There was never anybody else at that time in the little bar parlour, and apart from exchanging a few remarks with the landlady I spoke to nobody. I sprawled, my bones aching with tiredness, near the tiny window, through which the glow of the evening dimly filtered; and I alternated potato crisps with gulps of gin and tonic. There was as little to see as there was to say. It was all outwardly dull, and might even have been thought depressing. But after all the dodging about and fire and madness of London, the sirens and guns, the endless hours of excited talk in smoky basements, the split-second microphone business, the telephoning and type-writing, the loud rumours and mounting horrors, the cables and wires and letters, the flaming mid-nights seen with eyeballs of hot brass, this solitary mild tippling and nibbling without a thought in my head, only an unfathomable sense of peace and quiet and remoteness, soared above mere content to become delight, never to be forgotten, fit to be celebrated in something better than this prose, an hour of poetry....

10

Smoking as worship

I am told that in one of the ruined temples, deep in the jungle of Central America, there is a carving, more than two thousand years old, showing a Mayan priest smoking a pipe. It seems that the Mayans – bless them – used the smoke of tobacco as an offering to their sun god, who, more delicate in his tastes than most gods, relished this fragrant offering. So the Mayan priest, puffing away, was engaged in worship. And for more than thirty-five years, without knowing it, I have been a belated Mayan priest, following the ancient ritual of my order. Light Virginian and dark Burley, strong Perique and entrancing Latakia – I have sacrificed them all, by the pound and at monstrous prices, to the sun god. Possibly I have also sacrificed digestion, sleep, eyesight, nerves, and a final career as a Grand Old Man. I have no regrets. The sun god has been pleased, and I have known solace and sometimes delight.

Smoking as worship

There are those who call this a filthy habit. They should take a look at some of our other habits. For my part, even though the duty on tobacco mounts to such a height that I have to turn smuggler, I shall continue to sit in my own Central American jungle, bright with the birds of my fancy, still silently worshipping the sun god, offering him the dissolving blue shapes and the fragrance of my pipe.

11

Discovering Tomlinson

When I was in my teens in Bradford I found in the local paper some essays by H. M. Tomlinson, who afterwards included them, I fancy, in his travel book *The Sea and the Jungle*. And here I will call a short halt before recording the delight I felt. In those days, before 1914, a local newspaper could publish essays by Tomlinson. In the *Morning Post* and elsewhere you could find Belloc. For a halfpenny every Saturday you could buy the *Daily News* and Chesterton at his ripest. (It is only fair to add here that the Saturday *News Chronicle* still gives us Robert Lynd.) We are supposed to have made fine strides, with education and culture bounding forward, but where now do we find such writing in our newspapers? What prose does Fleet Street offer us now that we can set beside that of Belloc, Chesterton, Tomlinson, Beerbohm, Lucas, and the rest? What masters can a junior clerk with literary aspirations read now? Show me our pennyworths of superb prose. And don't talk to me of the paper shortage, for there is still room enough, it seems, for columns of rubbish. Let anybody search the pre-1914 files of the cheapest and most popular newspapers, and I will guarantee that he will find there more honest writing in a week's issues than he will find now in three years of such newspapers. And if this is true, then where, in this large field, is our progress? More children are in school, and stay there longer than they used to do, but outside the school door, waiting for applause, are the tired hacks of the contemporary Press, the cynical charlatans of the film, the second-rate mountebanks of the air. So where are we? But I am grumbling again.

So let me recall the delight I felt when I found among the wool prices and reports of Liberal meetings in our local *Observer* some strange pieces by one Tomlinson, headed *East and West of the Moon.* The magic of the title glittered all the way down the column. Three short sentences set me down in a far place, giving me there the eye of a falcon and a fine brooding mind. A full man, not a wool merchant or a Liberal politician, had been somewhere, and had returned to tell me what it was like there. Here in the morning paper, as fresh as the milk, was some *writing*. And to this day I am grateful to the author of it, H. M. Tomlinson, whose two masterpieces of travel, *The*

Sea and the Jungle and *Tidemarks*, have places of honour on my shelves. (I have other books of his, of course, but those two are supreme.) He has always seemed to me to be under-valued, and I agree with Wells in considering his account of the Tropics to be superior to Conrad's, more vivid and vital. He can still bring me delight after all these years. He is to me one of that tiny select group of writers whose work restores my own concern for our craft. Since I first stared at his essays in our morning paper I have often – all too often – been hasty and careless in my own prose (though I aim at a certain eagerness and sweep), but I think that without that early encounter with Tomlinson I would have been much worse. Bless you, Tommie!

12

And the Marx Brothers

One afternoon, nearly twenty years ago, some long-forgotten business took me to Golders Green, and when I had finished and was walking towards the Tube station there came a sudden drenching downpour. I had no raincoat, so I hurried into a cinema, more for shelter than for amusement. It was a large solemn cinema, almost empty, and I felt as quiet and remote in there as if I were sitting at the bottom of the sea. The news reel came and went. There were the usual fancy tricks with the lights. The feature film noisily arrived. I stared idly at the reception desk of an hotel in Florida. A fantastic character entered, and, without speaking a word, took the letters from the rack and casually tore them up, drank the ink, and began to eat the telephone. I sat up, lost in wonder and joy. The film was *The Cocoanuts*, and with it the Marx Brothers had entered my life. And this was the perfect way to discover these glorious clowns, unexpectedly in the middle of a wet afternoon in Golders Green. Since then – besides making their acquaintance and actually watching them on the job – I have followed them from cinema to cinema. I like them best when they are given the largest *carte blanche* – as in the sublime *Duck Soup* – but even when they are clamped to some miserable plot, have to give place to some preposterous tenor and his simpering girl, I do not desert them but sit there, waiting for such delight as they can offer me. My family – thank heaven – share this rapture, and we often exchange memories, mere shadows and echoes, of our favourite antics at the dinner table. Friends who refuse to enjoy these inspired zanies are regarded with suspicion. I have never understood why some London cinema does not show the Marx Brothers year in and year out. We appear to be living, as so many well-informed persons have observed, in a gigantic madhouse, but there are a few compensations even here, and one of them is that we have the Marx Brothers with us. Their clowning is a comment on our situation. Chico is the eternal, sulky but wistful peasant, sceptical but not without hope. Groucho is urban America, the office exec-utive, the speculator, the publicity agent, the salesman, raised to a height at which the folly of such men blazes like a beacon. Harpo is modern man with the lid off, a symbolic figure of the masculine unconscious. Together they have worked out comic routines that may be regarded one day as a saga of satire, Rabelais caught in celluloid. But even if they should be soon forgotten, some of us will remember how they dissolved us in laughter, during those evenings in the 'thirties when the fuses were already spluttering round our feet. Karl Marx showed us how the dispossessed would finally take possession. But I think the Brothers Marx do it better.

13

Cosy planning

Cosy planning. This can be delightful, and nobody I know has celebrated it. There should be two of you – or at most, three. Committees are out. So are strangers or acquaintances or even friends except the oldest and dearest. You need wives or husbands, parents or children. Late evening is the best time, and your own fireside the best place. What has to be planned can be a move, an elaborate holiday, some new enterprise. (If both planners are female, then weddings will do.) You draw close to the fire; one of you has paper and pencil, but there should not be much actual writing; the cold chaos of the world has retreated; you are both alert, business-like, know all manner of sensible tricks and dodges, are intent upon getting things done; but through all the pipes and channels of the plan there flows the warm current of your feeling for each other, and the whole business is securely and nourishingly rooted in a deep personal relationship. People who believe they are going there often wonder what they will do with themselves in Heaven. They make the mistake of assuming that the place will be all complete, finished to the last bit of gilding, before they arrive. But of course it won't be, and there will have to be lots of Cosy Planning.

14

Getting out of New York

New York is a city I can do nothing with. I cannot come to terms with it. I do not know what it means. I cannot discover the relation between the physical and spiritual scale of the place. All those temples without gods! A comic strip painted on vellum and bound in gold. On one visit I was taken up to a room in the clouds, a miracle of a room, and then had to listen to dreary bits of pornography. Broadway has more lights and more rubbish than any other street I know. And these incongruities defeat me. I swing between awe and contempt. In this city my feet are never solidly on the ground. For these and other reasons I am at my worst with New Yorkers, and they rarely seem to understand what I am saying or trying to do. Nevertheless, they keep me desperately busy when I am there. The telephone rings all the time. Sheafs of messages are waiting for me at the hotel. When at last I get to bed I am so exhausted that I cannot sleep. After a few days of this exhaustion and bewilderment I am a wreck of a man. Then comes the moment of delight. The hour arrives when I can board the long-distance train that will take me far away, to the mountains, to the desert, restoring to me the sensible earth; and here, deep in the honeycomb of the Grand Central, is the little compartment, my own place, where the African, solemn as a witch-doctor, is distributing my baggage; and now, after echoing Congo cries of warning, we are gliding away, escaping through this tunnel from the new Babel; and there will be no more telephone calls, urgent messages, interviews, noisy parties, and at any moment I shall be myself again. And although there is nothing to see yet but the dripping walls of a tunnel, it seems the most delightful journey in the world.

15

Buying music to escape tune-haunting

When I was younger – though it still happens occasionally now – I used to be haunted by tunes. They could come from anywhere – the *Quaker Girl* – or a late Beethoven quartet. They would haunt me for days on end, during which I would be performing in a kind of secret ballet to their accompaniment. Their rhythm became mine. Sometimes, and this was most maddening, I would find myself endlessly pursuing the theme, now catching it, now missing it. To rid myself of this obsession there was only one thing to be done. I had to buy the music, if it existed in a piano score (and there was always the gramophone for the quartets), and then hammer out the tune for myself. This always cured me. So away I would go to the music shop, and then hurry home with the piece securely rolled in paper. And that was the moment of delight – when I stood in front of the piano, hastily unrolling the music and then rolling it round the other way, so that it would behave itself on the music stand. Here, waiting with upturned face, was *La Belle Dame Sans Merci*, and, beyond her, freedom itself. A lad could hardly ask more from any moment of this time of ours.

16

Moment during rehearsal

Many playwrights enjoy attending performances of their own plays. Night after night will find them lurking at the back of the dress circle, and if they are discovered and challenged there they will pretend to be keeping an eye on old Brown, who plays the doctor, or deciding whether there could be a cut toward the end of Act Two. But – bless their hearts – they are really there to enjoy themselves. Now I am not one of these playwrights. Once a play is running smoothly I try to stay away from it. One reason is that I have given the production so much close study during the rehearsal period and have watched so carefully the first performances that I am weary of the piece and want to think about something else. If it is a serious play, I am more likely to be irritated than moved by it. If it is a comedy, then the sight and sound of the audience laughing do not make me think what a fine funny fellow I am, but arouse in me feelings of disgust. So there is no delight here for me. That comes much earlier, at some point during rehearsal. After the preliminary readings, which are interesting rather than delightful, you struggle along with moves and "business", and the actors put aside their scripts and try to remember their words; and all this for the author is rather like conducting a party of tourists across fields of glue. But then, if you are lucky, there comes a moment when – suddenly, miraculously – the play is alive. There is no set, no lights, no costumes and make-up, no effects, no audience, yet perhaps the play is more alive than it ever will be again for you. You forget that you are still messing about with chairs and orange-boxes and chalklines on an empty stage lit with one glaring bulb. You forget the cleaners still chattering and banging in the upper circle, and the empties that are being noisily taken out of the stalls bar. You forget the traffic roaring outside. You forget that this theatre has merely been lent to you until five o'clock, and that as yet you have no theatre of your own. You forget all these things because now a miracle happens. The stage manager and his assistant, seated at their familiar table, marking the prompt script, fade from your consciousness. The horrible "working light" is no longer there; strange dawns or exquisite sunsets appear. The chalklines and orange-boxes turn into walls and tables and sofas, all perfect. Miss

Thing, wearing her oldest clothes, her hair anyhow, with pinched features and a yellow complexion, suddenly transforms herself into the beautiful creature of your imagination. Young So-and-so – up to now a lout and a bad bit of casting – flashingly emerges as a gay and handsome breaker of hearts. Old Whose-it, who seemed to be a mistake, if only because he drinks too much and cannot remember a line, is now your lovable Old Smith to the last wrinkle and chuckle. And what pathos – what comedy – what suspense – that truth to life – what profound symbolism! Yes, it is here – as you first imagined it – no, better – much better – oh glory! Only for a few minutes at best; but while it lasts, this transfiguration, what delight!

17

Sound of a football

When I was a boy I lived in a new suburb with playing fields not far away. During the holidays we would pick sides for football, always soccer, and play all day. We might have different meal-times – rushing home to dinner any time between twelve and two – but this only made the daylong game easier to manage. We would arrive home, breathless and scarlet, put away two or three help-ings of suet pudding, and then hurry back to the game. (Am I suffering for it now, in middle-age? I doubt it. And as for most of the others, they never reached their middle twenties but died among the shell holes and barbed wire on July 1st, 1916.) In the morning, in the afternoon, in the early evening, as I went clattering in my football boots, past the row of half-built houses towards the field, I would hear the thud-thud-thud of the ball, a sound unlike any other, and delight would rise in my heart.

There are moments even now, forty years afterwards, when I find myself in some country lane and hear that thud-thud-thud, that unmistakable call to the field, and I feel an itching in my insteps and for a daft fraction of a second I imagine the game is still there for me to join, forgetting how the years have gone and that I am now a heavy ageing man. But before the tide of regret sweeps over my mind, the grey and salty tide, there sparkles, like some treasure on the sand, not some mere memory of past pleasure but, for a flashing quarter-second, the old delight itself.

18

Romantic recognition

Romantic recognition. Two examples will do. When we were flying from Erivan, the capital of Armenia, to Sukhum, on the Black Sea, a Soviet scientist, who spoke English, tapped me on the shoulder and then pointed to a fearsome rock face, an immeasurable slab bound in the iron of eternal winter. "That," he announced, "is where Prometheus was chained." And then all my secret terror – for a journey among the mountains of the Caucasus in a Russian plane is to my unheroic soul an ordeal – gave way for a moment to wonder and delight, as if an illuminated fountain had shot up in the dark. And then, years earlier, in the autumn of 1914, when we were on a route march in Surrey, I happened to be keeping step with the company commander, an intelligent Regular lent to us for a month or two. We were passing a little old woman who was watching us from an open carriage, drawn up near the entrance to a mansion. "Do you know who that is?" the captain asked; and of course I didn't. "It's the Empress Eugenie," he told me; and young and loutish as I was in those days, nevertheless there flared about me then, most delightfully, all the splendour and idiocy of the Second Empire, and I knew that we, every man Jack of us, were in history, and knew it once and for all.

19

Old photograph

A photograph can do it, even a photograph without any personal associations. I cannot remember when and where I first saw Mrs. Cameron's photograph of the young Ellen Terry, but I know that then and there, ever since and everywhere, it has never failed to bring me delight. The girl herself, as she leans there with closed eyes, her right hand clutching at her necklace, her nose perfect in its tilted witty imperfection, is of course very beautiful, a lass unparalleled. But that is only the beginning. No doubt the long curve of neck and shoulder, catching the light, is exquisite. But though the aesthetic values are there, it is not they that do the trick. There is the fact that here, so suddenly confronting us, is the youth of somebody whom men of my generation think of in her old age; for here she is, that lioness, as she was nearly thirty years before I was born. And she is not only young Ellen Terry or madcap little Mrs. Watts, she is Woman herself, her soul withdrawn behind those heavy eyelids, the mystery, the challenge, the torment, the solace. Yet it would not be all the same if this were not a photograph but a painting or drawing, some other man's vision. That would be art, but this, however artfully the sitter has been posed and the camera handled, is an objective record. This is how she was, on such a day, and not how she sang in some man's brain. But though a photograph indeed, this is an old old photograph, taken a long lifetime ago, with everybody who first admired it dead and gone. It is a legacy too from some tiny golden age of photography, some pure and massive Old Kingdom of lens and plate, of autumnal sunlight and sepia shadows. And all these facts and fancies, unrecognised at the time and only to be discovered and disengaged by analysis, come furiously crowding into the mind as our eyes meet this photograph; and because there is such a stir of them, then delight follows at once. Yes, even a photograph can do it.

20

Coming home

I am not impressed by the raptures of homecoming travellers when they single out the white cliffs, the comfortable slopes of the Downs, the dazzling scribble of buttercups and daisies outside the train windows; for when I have been some time away from England, then even what I usually dislike here can bring me a flash of delight. I welcome with joy the glum railway sidings, the platforms that exist in a perpetual November, the *Daily Piffler* and the *Weekly Blatherer* on the bookstalls, the mournful muck of the refreshment room, the gimcrack bungalows, the little towns that have never once been gay and gaudy, the hoardings given up to second-rate musical comedies, the vast gloom and decay of London. What a civilisation! What a mess! What a country! But I'm home ... I'm home....

21

Smell of Tahiti

Our noses can do it for us. You turn into some side street where they are roasting coffee in the morning, or you pass a baker's on a winter's night – and immediately you nose out delight. But perhaps the most satisfying and also the most romantic smell is that of Earth itself. That time, for instance, when we were approaching Tahiti. We had sailed from San Francisco in an old New Zealand mail steamer, whose captain, dourly determined to entertain his passengers, used to read to us jokes and riddles from his favourite Wellington weekly. Soon we lost the Earth, for the Pacific Ocean is even larger than it appears to be on the map. We saw no land, no passing ships, and even the seabirds vanished. For days we appeared to be cutting our way through purple-black marble, thinly veined with foam. After that the sun of the cursed Ancient Mariner glared down on us, set up noons of hot brass, and drained our hollow globe of all colour. As we crossed the equator, I took to shivering, as if lost in some sudden little winter of my own; my temperature jumped to a hundred and five; I departed for Delirium; and then, returning to the ship, existed shakily on jugs of iced orangeade and tinned asparagus, which I have never tasted since without a shudder of the palate. When I was allowed on deck again, it was only to discover that nothing had changed except our position on the map. There were the sun, the dissolving blues and melting meaningless distances, the mild waste of waters. Earth might have gone for ever; perhaps there were no people left alive except ourselves; we were churning our way out of Time itself; we had joined the Flying Dutchman, with not even a riddle left from the Wellington weekly. This was not a voyage but another life, gradually thinning out into a long vague dream. And then it happened, without anybody warning us. There was nothing to see, not even a thickening of the southern horizon: it was our noses that discovered the coming landfall. No doubt this smell that brought us such delight was compounded of copra, decayed fish, frangi-panni and vanilla, oil and sweat, stew and fries, dung and blossom; but there it was, this Earth of ours; and while we hung eagerly over the rail, sniffing away, seeing nothing, hearing nothing, our happy noses already began to land on the South Sea Isles.

22

Chamber music at home

Chamber music at home is delightful. Not for everybody of course; mere listeners, passive guest types, may have a hell of a time with it. (Let them go somewhere else and switch on their Third Programme.) No, this kind of music is delightful for actual performers, and for those who are loitering round the edge of performance, waiting to be asked to join in, and for those women – and a few wise men – who enjoy seeing the persons dear to them happy, let the notes fall where they may. There has always been to me a sort of cosy magic about it. (In *Bright Day* I made a musical family a symbol of magical attraction.) You are at home, all safe and snug, and yet are also wandering in spirit, through lost kingdoms, with the music. Even the best string quartets and trios will not always survive the atmosphere, chilly with determined culture, of those horrible little concert halls given up to chamber music.

There is too a concert solemnity, as German as liver sausage, that blights many of the sauciest trifles. (We forget that a lot of music has been written *for fun*.) What a difference when you bring in firelight, armchairs, tobacco, and a tray of drinks! The execution – as it often is with us – may be sketchy and even downright murderous, but you can catch the mood of the masters, whether they are looking for the Holy Grail or a pint of wine and a helping of roast goose. (I fancy, though, that the late Beethoven quartets ought to be left out of the home programme.) You wish you could do it better, but you are delighted to be doing it at all. When, for example, Mary (violin) and her friend Joan ('cello) and I (piano more or less) gave up most of a recent week-end to our struggle with the Smetana trio, I doubt if in any but the slowest passages I was hitting more than half the proper notes in the treble or a third of those in the bass; but the girls, aloft on their professional standard, enjoyed it, and as for me, floundering and grunting and sweating, I would not have missed a minute of it for a hundred pounds. Bestriding the hacked corpse of poor Smetana, I drank the milk of paradise. We had no audience, and needed none, but went off, morning and night, into the Bohemian blue together. But I need not perform myself, nor be in my own home, to know this delight. As I write this, many rooms come flickering back, in Bradford and Cambridge, a Lakeland cottage, a studio in Chelsea, half-forgotten mysterious apartments abroad; and firelight and candle-light play tenderly among the instruments; and Mozart and Haydn, Brahms and Debussy, move among us again; and within the ring of friendly faces, ghosts these many years, the little worlds of sound shine and revolve like enchanted moons. Why – bless our bewildered souls! – every time a violin is taken up to the lumber room, a piano is carted away, and in their place is a gadget that turns music on and off like tap water, we move another step away from sanity and take to snarling harder than ever.

23

Charades

Playing charades. Showing off came into it, naturally; for I thought I was good at charades (and so I was too); but there was, throughout all that desperate improvisation, usually in the hall with too many people merely trying things on and giggling, and throughout the clowning that followed in the drawing-room, a reaching out toward something only half-realised in oneself. Our favourite scene at home when I was a boy was the Fat Men Scene, which had to be brought in somehow, as even I, with my sterner standard of the game, admitted; and indeed I would not have allowed it to be overlooked. My father and some of his friends needed only a few cushions to be magnificent Fat Men, while I and my like took to pillows and overcoats, and blew out our cheeks until we dissolved, as we always did very soon, into laughter. The antics were simple indeed, and followed a familiar recipe; but all of us, even the stateliest wives of deacons, laughed until we cried. And now, forty years afterwards, I am a Fat Man, without the help of a single cushion; and every night, on twenty stages, in places I have never seen, they play my charades. But where – oh where – is that old delight?

24

My first article

When I was sixteen I was already writing articles and offering them to any kind of editor whose address I could discover. These articles were of two kinds. The first, which I signed portentously "J. Boynton Priestley", were serious, very serious indeed, and were full of words like "renaissance" and "significance" and "aftermath", and suggested that their author was about a hundred and fifty years old. And nobody wanted them. They could not be given away. No editor had a body of readers old enough for such articles. The other kind were skits and burlesques and general funny work, written from the grimly determined humorous standpoint of the school magazine. One of these was accepted, printed and paid for by a London humorous weekly. I had arrived. (And my father, not to be found wanting on such an occasion, presented me with one of his fourpenny cigars, with which, as I fancy he guessed, I had been secretly experimenting for some months.) The issue of the weekly containing my article burst upon the world. Riding inside a tram from Duckworth Lane to Godwin Street, Bradford, I saw a middle-aged woman opening this very copy of the weekly, little knowing, as I made haste to tell myself, that one of its group of brilliant contributors was not two yards away. I watched her turn the pages. She came to *the* page; she hesitated; she stopped, she began to read my article. Ah – what delight! But mine, of course, not hers. And not mine for long, not more than a second, for then there settled on her face an expression I have noticed ten thousand times since, and have for years now tried not to notice – the typical expression of the reader, the audience, the customer, the patron. How shall I describe this curious look? There is in it a kind of innocence – and otherwise I think I would have stopped writing years ago – but mixed a trifle sourly with this admirable innocence is a flavouring of wariness, perhaps a touch of suspicion itself. "Well, what have we here?" it enquires dubiously. And then the proud and smirking Poet and Maker falls ten thousand feet into dubiety. So ever since that tram ride I have never caught a glimpse of the reader, the audience, the customer, the patron, without instantly trying to wedge myself into the rocks above the black tarn of doubt. As I do this, there is the flash of a blue wing – and the bird of delight has flown.

25

Celebrating at parties

When I first settled in London, in the early nineteen-twenties, it was still the fashion for literary hostesses to give very large evening parties, to which all manner of writers, old or young, famous or unknown, were invited. There is much to be said for this form of hospitality. The cocktail party, given at an hour when honest men should still be working, has proved a wretched substitute for it. At the old evening parties, when the day's work was done, there was time for real conversation and you got to know people there. There was space too for the big guns and little guns, lions and mice. Literature itself, I suspect, gained because young writers were able to meet their famous elders. The fierce young critic, denouncing all established reputations, turned out to be a bashful homely lad with a pretty wife. The established reputation proved himself to be something better and far more formidable

than a pompous old fraud. Personalities were appreciated; views were exchanged; and all at a late convivial
hour when a genial tolerance was in the air. It is quite
possible that the disappearance of these parties, and the
consequent lack of any spacious meeting ground for old
and young writers, the established and the newly arrived,
has helped to disintegrate, almost to atomise, our literary
life. And certainly their absence has robbed newcomers to
London, the lads who are now in the position I was in
1922, of one peculiar bit of delight. This came from
suddenly finding oneself in the same room as the celebri-
ties of one's profession. There you were – the fellow-guest
of giants, of figures that were almost mythological. There
they were – eating and drinking and chattering, solid
beings existing in the same world. If it came to a push –
though you would be well advised not to try – you could
actually offer a whisky-and-soda and a ham sandwich to
Bernard Shaw. Just when the voice of H. G. Wells was
rising to a *coloratura* height of derision, you could crash
in and contradict him. You could steal up to Arnold
Bennett and whisper balefully that he was old-fashioned.
There was nothing, except your reverence for that
commanding personage, to prevent your asking W. B.
Yeats to use his imagination. Belloc and Chesterton, in
full stride over the Pyrenees and blowing the horn of
Roland, could be halted with a demand for them to define

their terms. None of these would have been wise moves, but they could have been made, as you realised to your delight, just because there, not two plates of sandwiches away, they were, the genuine monsters themselves. I will admit that the circumstances were different then. Our literary values were more stable. As a youngster, before 1914, I had read and revered these writers, who occupied far more space, just because there was more space to spare in those easy old days, than any writers do now. It was much easier then to create the legends. Their figures had not to be seen against today's towering background, lit with hellfire, of world drama. The stage on which they played was domestic and cosy. Even cartoonists then still had time and space for literary men. Those were years not of grim action but of debate, which explains why born debaters like Shaw and Chesterton, encouraged by a Press that had room for everything, were so often standing in the limelight. No literary youngster now could find – parties or no parties – giants so famous, because his boyish imagination would not have been at work so long building them up. Thus his delight could never be equal to mine. And it was not just snobbery. It was more subtle and more profound than that. It came, I think, from a feeling, flashing through the mind like a silver arrow, that the world had been suddenly and miraculously enlarged, that legend and reality rushed together and became one.

Imagine a hostess saying: "I'm so glad you could come. Now who would you like to meet? Haroun al Raschid? Falstaff? Don Quixote? Mr. Pickwick?" Yes, it was nearly as good as that, attending a literary party in the early 'Twenties; and I am not ashamed to declare that I gaped and stammered in delight.

26

Making writing simple

At the end of a long talk with a youngish critic, a sincere fellow whose personality (though not his values) I respect, he stared at me and then said slowly: "I don't understand you. Your talk is so much more complicated – subtle – than your writing. Your writing always seems to me too simple." And I replied: "But I've spent years and years trying to make my writing simple. What you see as a fault, I regard as a virtue." There was now revealed to us the gulf between his generation and mine. He and his lot, who matured in the early 'thirties, wanted literature to be difficult. They grew up in revolt against the Mass Communication antics of their age. They did not want to share anything with the crowd. Writing that was hard to understand was like a password to their secret society. A good writer to them was one who made his readers toil and sweat. They admired extreme cleverness and solemnity, poets like political cardinals, critics who came to literature like specialists summoned to a consultation at a king's bedside. A genuine author, an artist, as distinct from hacks who tried to please the mob, began with some simple thoughts and impressions and then proceeded to complicate his account of them, if only to keep away the fools. Difficulty was demanded: hence the vogue of Donne and Hopkins. Literature had to respond to something twisted, tormented, esoteric, in their own secret natures. In all this there was no pose; and here their elders went wrong about them. They could be accused not unjustly of narrowness and arrogance, but not of insincerity. They were desperately sincere in believing that the true artist must hide from the crowd behind a thicket of briers. They grew up terrified of the crowd, who in this new Mass Age seemed to them to be threatening all decent values. But I was born in the nineteenth century and my most impressionable years were those just before 1914. Rightly or wrongly, I am not afraid of the crowd. And art to me is not synonymous with introversion. (I regard this as the great critical fallacy of our time.) Because I am what is called now "an intellectual" – and I am just as much "an intellectual" as these younger chaps – I do not feel that there is a glass wall between me and the people in the nearest factories, shops and pubs. I do not believe that my thoughts and feelings are quite different from theirs. I prefer therefore a wide channel of communication. Deliberately I aim at simplicity and not complexity in my writing. No matter what the subject in hand might be, I want to write something that at a pinch I could read aloud in a bar-parlour. (And the time came when I was heard and understood in a thousand bar-parlours.) I do not pretend to be subtle and profound, but when I am at work I try to appear simpler than I really am. Perhaps I make it too easy for the reader, do too much of the toiling and sweating myself. No doubt I am altogether too obvious for the cleverest fellows, who want to beat their brains against something hard and knotty. But then I am not impressed by this view of literature, as a cerebral activity. Some contemporary critics would be better occupied solving chess problems and breaking down cyphers. They are no customers of mine, and I do not display my goods to catch their eye. But any man who thinks the kind of simplicity I attempt is easy should try it for himself, if only in his next letter to *The Times*. I find it much easier now than I used to do, but that is because I have kept this aim in view throughout years of hard work. I do not claim to have achieved even now a prose that is like an easy persuasive voice, preferably my own at its best; but this is what I have been trying to do for years, quite deliberately, and it is this that puzzled my friend, the youngish critic, who cannot help wanting something quite different. And this habit of simplification has its own little triumphs. Thus, I was asked to pay a birthday tribute, on the air, to C. G. Jung, for whose work and personality I have a massive admiration. To explain Jung in thirteen-and-a-half minutes so that the ordinary listener could understand what the fuss was about! My friends said it could not be done. The psychologists said it could not be done. But I can reasonably claim, backed by first-class evidence, that I did it. It was a tough little task but when I had come to the end of it, I found, like honey in the rock, a taste of delight.

27

Books and music and furnished houses

I cannot pretend to be sorry that we no longer have to rent furnished houses for the children's holidays. Yet one bit of delight is missing. This came from rummaging through other people's books and music. The collections were always odd, because people who let their houses have rarely accumulated fine libraries of books and music; but the very oddity of the stuff they left behind for you added to the charm of these new possessions. Under the piano stool or in a neighbouring cupboard would be Field's "Nocturnes", pot-pourris from Meyerbeer, roaring "galops" arranged for duet, selections from "San Toy" and "The Earl and the Girl", and all the tinkling nonsense of my youth, such as "In the Shadows" or "Glow-worm". And after breakfast and before it was time to go down to the beach, you could light a pipe and bang away at the yellow keys. The books, all jammed into one small book-case, would probably include Rider Haggard and Seton Merriman in paper backs, nice little Tushery historical romances in Nelson's sevenpenny series, and perhaps Ouida or Trollope or Clark Russell or Charles Reade in the yellow-backed old Chatto and Windus cheap editions, opening with formidable advertisements of Beecham's pills and Keating's powder. For these the serious reading, so carefully selected for the holiday, would instantly be abandoned. The beds were uncomfortable, the chairs dubious, the plate and linen a mere laughable sketch, and the whole house an enterprise soon regretted; but for the first day or two – what fun the books and music were!

28

Shakespeare
re-discovered

If I were kidnapped, taken to the Oxford or Cambridge Union, and told I must either debate a motion or be thrown into the river, I would propose: *That Shakespeare is the curse – and may prove the ruin – of the English Theatre.* For the Bard keeps popping up everywhere, and does no good to anybody in the professional Theatre. Managers do not mind him, because he asks for no royalties (if they had to pay him ten per cent of the gross, they would begin to wonder about him); he is Culture and a possible grant from the Arts Council; and you can always run extra matinees for the schoolchildren. Actors like him because they can gum on a lot of crêpe hair, bellow almost anything that comes into their heads, and then have their *King Lear* taken seriously by the critics. Actors have only to persist in playing the chief Shakespearean roles, and, although they may be so bad that I would not allow them to bring on a telegram in a play of mine, very soon they are regarded as ornaments of Our Stage and are given a civic lunch in Coketown. Leading actresses love Shakespeare because they started off with him at school and the Royal Academy of Dramatic Art, and adore wearing fancy costumes and using that smudgy breathy technique. And from neither sex is required any sharp outlining of character, any close observation of real life. If you offer the people in front a performance as a bank manager or a charwoman, those people have some notion of when you are hitting or missing the mark; but give them dim remote queens or armoured barons in blank verse and you are safe from genuine criticism. Whether most producers like doing Shakespeare, I have never been able to decide; but they set to work on him as if they hated the ubiquitous old William, as if the only thing to do with the Swan of Avon was to wring its neck. The result is nearly always the Theatre at its silliest. All that ranting and cooing, that guffawing and back-slapping, that comic business which would be thrown out of a third-rate touring pantomime! Oh - those anaemic sighing maidens and roaring gallants, all wondering what they are saying; those neighing, chin-stroking clowns; those idiotic messengers from the battlefields! Oh – dear, dear, dear!

And yet once we are no longer clamped on to a heavy-handed production by the pro's, when we come unexpectedly upon the smiling poet himself, what delight he gives us! One night we switch on the wireless and instead of a portentous talk, a half-wit's joke, or erotic laments from the swamp, we hear with up-rising hair –

> O, wither'd is the garland of the war,
> The soldiers' pole is fall'n: young boys and girls
> Are level now with men; the odds is gone,
> And there is nothing left remarkable
> Beneath the visiting moon....

Or we visit a school at half-term and in the packed oven of the gymnasium, where the play is being performed, we recognise in the four-foot-nine figure of *Charles the Wrestler* one of the scarlet-faced boys whose giant tea we paid for at the "White Horse"; and then hear him pipe up, as unconcerned as a lark:

... They say he is already in the forest of Arden, and a many merry men with him; and there they live like the old Robin Hood of England; they say many young gentlemen flock to him every day, and fleet the time carelessly, as they did in the golden world....

And – crikey! – call him Shakespeare, Bacon, Essex, Southampton or Uncle Tom Cobbley – what a chap!

29

The conductors

The conductors ... when I was a boy – massive old Richter commanding the massive old Hallé ... then that night, when it was as if electricity had just been discovered, Nikisch arrived with the London Symphony – a man in a tranced white passion ... the noble silvery Bruno Walter, transmuting Wagner into sunlight, green leaves, bird-song ... the first amazed hearing of Toscanini and his New York Philharmonic, with everything at once solid and soaring, mathematics and magic Tommy Beecham, duelling for Mozart with a glittering rapier ... and the enraptured de Sabata, taking the whole London Philharmonic with him up the steps to Beethoven's heaven, and there frenziedly beating with his fists upon the vast invisible doors ... why, my dear *maestros*, in spite of wars, bombs, taxes, rubbish and all, what a delight it has been to share this world and age with you!

30

Theatre curtains

Delicate scornful young gentlemen who I lecture on the Drama at our universities always refer contemptuously to our picture-frame stage of today and are decided in their preference for the open Elizabethan stage. (They seem to think that if Shakespeare had been offered a modern switchboard he would have turned it down. Like hell he would!) These choice spirits are all for rough-and-tumble popular stuff so long as it is a few safe centuries away. I doubt if many of them are ever to be found in the gallery of Collin's Music Hall or at an All-in Wrestling match. But perhaps the Victoria Palace or the Palladium then? Again, I doubt it. But although the picture-frame stage, with its relentless barrier of the proscenium arch (through which I in my time have tried, at some expense, to escape, and so far without the support of a single University lecturer on the Drama), has its faults, it does give us unfailingly one delightful moment. That is the moment when the "House Lights" have faded out, and the "floats", which is our professional English term for the footlights, have been turned up; so that all is darkness except where the lower folds of the heavy velvet curtain are expectantly and most enchantingly catching the light. It is a tiny hushed dawn. It might be another avatar. Nothing stirs for a second except our imagination. What do those lighted folds conceal? What lies behind that rich October morning of the velvet? And perhaps it is then, just before the curtain trembles and rises, that we should leave the theatre.

31

Fantastic theories

A first encounter with any grand fantastic theory, not political or economic, delights me. There are not enough of them. I wish we had more bold men like Mr. H. S. Bellamy, who believes – and has a lovely time with his belief – that the moon is merely the last of a series of small planets captured by the earth; that the final disintegration of the previous moon brought about an appalling catastrophe, the rumours of which still reach us through myths, folk tales, and the Book of Revelations; that the golden age was the quiet tideless time between moons; and that the arrival of our present satellite, about thirteen thousand years ago, gave us the Flood. Mr. Bellamy is my Ancient Mariner; I can never decide whether he is offering me profound new truths or the wildest nonsense; but he is one of my favourite writers – and long may he flourish! I have had my happy hours too with the late Charles Fort, the American who thumbed his nose at all the sciences, crammed whole volumes with records of inexplicable events and seeming miracles, and concluded magnificently that "Something is using us." But that Something is not leaving us enough of these theorists; and I fear that there will not be many new specimens to delight me in my old age. Atlantis now. We have heard nothing from there lately, except by way of the planchette; and I care nothing for this spiritualist stuff, mere ectoplasm. What I like is a whacking great romantic theory, a tale as tall as any by Rider Haggard (and how good he was!), all carefully dressed, in black coat and striped trousers, to look like a thesis offered to and accepted by the British Association. Spiritualists, Theosophists, and all young women who were once high priestesses of the twelfth dynasty will not do. Otherwise, I will undertake to go halfway to meet anybody with fresh news of Atlantis. (I never cared for Lemuria.) The notion of atomic energy – misused, I'll be bound, by the followers of the Dark Gods on the middle island of Atlantis – ought to be inspiring somebody. So I shall not despair. At this very hour, some elderly engineer who had a bad go of sunstroke, some retired sea captain, with the moon still entangled in his rigging, may be just completing an eighty-thousand-word volume, outwardly as sedate as a bank inspector, that will suddenly flower for me into a fantastic theory; and I shall sit up late at night with it, looking uncommonly like stout Cortez.

32

Smoking in hot bath

Lying in a hot bath, smoking a pipe. And Elagabalus himself, after driving his white horses through the gold-dusted streets of Rome, never knew anything better; nor indeed anything as good, not having either pipe or tobacco. People still say to me "The way you work!", and behind the modest smirk I laugh secretly, knowing myself to be one of the laziest and most self-indulgent men alive. Long after they have caught the 8.20, opened the morning mail, telephoned to the managing director of the Cement Company, dictated yet another appeal to the Board of Trade, I am lying in my hot bath, smoking a pipe. I am not even soaping and scrubbing, but simply lying there, like a pink porpoise, puffing away. In a neighbouring room, thrown on the floor, are the morning papers, loud with more urgent demands for increased production, clamouring for every man and woman to save the country. And there I am, lost in steam, the fumes of Latakia, and the vaguest dreams. Just beyond the bolted door, where the temperature drops to nearly freezing point, are delicate women, who have already been up for hours, toiling away. And do I care? Not a rap. Sometimes I pretend, just to test the credulity of the household, that I am planning my day's work; but I am doing nothing of the kind. Often I do not intend to do any work at all during the day; and even when I know I must do some, I could not possibly plan it, in or out of a bath. No, I am just lying there, a pampered slug, with my saurian little eyes half-closed, cancelling the Ice Ages, lolling again in the steamy hot morning of the world's time, wondering dimly what is happening to Sir Stafford Cripps. "... One of the most energetic and prolific of our authors...." *Gertcha!*

33

A bit of writing

This is always happening: the discovery or re-discovery of a bit of real writing. Jack Horner work – you put in a thumb. For example, this morning I wanted a book, any book, and my hand fell on Tennyson's *Idylls of the King*, which I have not read for years and years. The book opened at Merlin and Vivien, and I read –

... He was mute:
So dark a forethought roll'd about his brain,
As on a dull day in an Ocean cave
The blind wave feeling round his long sea-hall
In silence ...

And I stared in delight, my mind possessed by the evocative image of the blind wave. Living as I do not far from Tennyson's old home, I know every silly story about the vain old monster, but immediately they are cancelled out, forgotten, and the seedy Victorian lion becomes a magician, another Merlin, and I salute him in gratitude, admiration and wonder. For if any man thinks it is easy to write like that – let him sit down and try it.

34

Walk in pine wood

Near the house, high on a hill, were woods of pine and fir; and, slipping away from the others, I followed a path that led me into one of these woods, through a tunnel of green gloom and smoky blue dusk. It was very quiet, very remote, in there. My feet sank into the pile of the pine needles. The last bright tatters of sunlight vanished. Some bird went whirring and left behind a deeper silence. I breathed a different air, ancient and aromatic. I had not gone a hundred paces before I had walked out of our English South-country and was deep in the Northern forest itself, with a thickness of time, centuries and centuries of it, pressing against me. Little doors at the back of my mind were softly opened. It was not the mere quickening of fancy that brought me delight then, but an atavistic stirring and heightening of the imagination, as if all my distant ancestors, who were certainly of the North, were whispering and pointing in this sudden dusk. Any turn now might bring me to the magical smithy, the cave of the dragon; a horn might blow and shatter the present time like so much painted glass; the world of legend, hung about these trees like the spiders' webs, was closing round me. No doubt my precious ego, challenged at every step, felt a touch of fear; but my true self, recognising this enlargement of life, finding its place for a moment or two in that procession which is the real life of Man, drew deeper breaths, lived in its own world during these moments, and was delighted.

35

Answering back

Answering Back – when you have a beautiful clear case. One example will do. During the war when I was broadcasting a great deal and received many letters of abuse, an angry gentleman from South Devon wrote something to this effect: "It is about time you realised that many of us are sick and tired of your references in broadcasts and articles to *The Old School Tie*. Even you ought to understand that by this time we have had more than enough of it –" etc., etc. I replied: "I am interested to learn that you are sick and tired of my repeated references to *The Old School Tie*. No doubt you will also be interested to learn that in no broadcast or article have I ever mentioned *The Old School Tie*, as this happens to be a term that I have always deliberately refrained from using." Delight? Certainly.

36

Manly talk

Bluff manly talk, with a big background of travel and adventure behind it, like the old *Wide World Magazine*; and with everybody pretending to be a Kipling character. The best setting for it used to be the smoke-rooms of smaller liners. What are you having? Another large pink?… Ever been up the Orinoco?… No, that wasn't Staggers, that was his brother, the old China hand… Spent a Christmas Day once in Port Limon – hot as hell!… Didn't I run into you once at Charlie's bar?… Have the other half, old boy?… Made a packet in Jo'burg, nobody knows how. … Not a gun I ever cared for.… Bet him a dam' good dinner at Scott's that he couldn't. … Bloke I used to fish with always sends me a case. … Skipper was plastered all the time and he put us in at Benguella.… Steward, four Mumbo-Jumbos - and don't forget the dash. … Yes, that was Moppy Philips - what a lad! - ran off with his C.O.'s wife.… Got it in Bangkok one time, but it's a long story. … What about one for the road? Hey, George!…

37

Frightening civil servants

Frightening senior civil servants. This may seem a cruel sport, sadistic delight; but there is some excuse for me, if not for you, because I am the kind of man nearly all senior civil servants dislike on sight; and indeed some of them dislike me, I gather, even without seeing me. To work, then. First, select your man, preferably one who if he does not make a mistake is about to be promoted or given a title; and then outline to him, with plenty of rhetoric and some magnificent gestures, a huge crazy scheme that will not only involve his department but also tangle him up with half-a-dozen other departments. Hint that some very influential personages are already enthusiastic about this scheme, but mention no names. Sweep away, like the rubbish they are, his objections. Enlarge grandly upon one of the unsoundest details of the scheme. Then when he protests with more vigour, suddenly change your tactics. Banish all smiles, large gestures, warmly enthusi-astic tones. Become the coldly hostile intriguer. Stare at him as long as you and he can bear it. When you speak again, be careful to mention his name and, if possible, his official position. "So, Mr. Clibtree," you say sourly, "as assistant secretary in charge of Snarks and Boojums in the Ministry of Jabber-wocky, you are entirely opposed to this scheme, are you?" Then nod several times, make an entry in a pocket-book, mutter something about the Press and Questions in the House, declare in a louder tone that you are busy, already late for a more important engage-ment, give him a last grim smile and march straight out. Delightful? Perhaps not.

38

Fiddling while Rome burns

Fiddling while Rome burns. In the morning I finished Vogt's *Road to Survival*, of which the publisher had sent me an advance copy. The argument – that as the world's population increases, our supply of arable land decreases, so that we are rushing toward disaster – was not new; but Vogt, in a fine frenzy, rushes you from continent to continent, shouting his news of soil erosion and dwindling water supplies and mounting hungry populations, until you see nothing in the future but wars, famine and death. Then, after writing to the publisher to commend this urgent call for a last-minute planetary S.O.S., I went into town to get a haircut, discovered some old pianola rolls in a music shop, and returned home to play them. I had thirty-minutes of pure delight, pedalling away at jazz of the best period – "The Doll Dance", "Tiptoe Through the Tulips", "Piccolo Pete" – and the rest. As the delicious nonsense was hammered out in the pianola's silver and bronze – I bring a light hand and foot to these affairs, let me tell you, and turn them out all crisp and sparkling – I was enjoying the tunes and enjoying various dreamlike fragmentary memories of when and where I had first heard them. Our daft species was hell-bent for starvation and ruin. Never had the future looked worse. And I knew, I knew. But there I was, pedalling away, my mind jiggling with the keys, a sound progressive man in his middle fifties, not giving – for thirty minutes or so – a damn.

39

Family silliness, domestic clowning

Family silliness, domestic clowning. This cannot be described in any detail, and it would be disastrous to quote even the best of the jokes. A fairly large family is necessary, but nobody concerned need have any great sense of humour. You start with any bit of nonsense, usually at the dining table, and then everybody adds shaggy pieces of their own, until the whole table is roaring and screaming and the scarlet cheeks of the younger children are wet with tears of laughter. To a sensitive outsider the scene would bring no delight at all, and indeed would probably seem repulsive. But then it is not meant for outsiders, sensitive or otherwise. You have to be thoroughly in it and *of* it to appreciate its quality. Somewhere below this rowdy monkey business are deep hidden roots, and somewhere above it are invisible blossoms. A collective personality springs into being some time during this slapstick. Without a happy togetherness, the little farce would never begin. And it is scenes like these, without dignity, real wit or beauty, made up of screeching and bellowing and fourth-rate jokes about treacle puddings or castor oil, that a man who feels his life ebbing out may recall with an anguish of regret and tenderness, remembering as if it were a lost bright kingdom the family all at home and being silly.

40

New box of matches

In the early 'Twenties, when I was writing regularly for the *London Mercury*, I used to spend much time, and far too much money, in the pub below in Poppins Court. Among the company there was a dark, romantic-Regency sort of man called Bohun Lynch, who did a very brave thing, for he wrote a novel about happiness. (He died not long afterwards, and it may be that his unconscious mind, prompting him to write this novel, already knew that Death was hurrying to meet him.) It was called *A Perfect Day*, and it was crammed with as many felicities as poor Lynch could muster for his hero. I have forgotten most of the novel, but I always remember that this hero of his found himself picking up a brand-new box of matches and experiencing a definite sensuous pleasure at the sight and feel of it. I knew what he meant; and ever since, when

I have picked up a new box of matches and known a tiny flicker of delight, I have remembered Bohun Lynch, and have caught a glimpse again of his dark, romantic-Regency face.

41

Playing with small children

When I am playing with small children (and I am an old and cunning hand) I do all those things that bore or irritate me in my adult life. For example, I plunge, to their delight and mine, into ritual and tradition, create secret societies, arrange elaborate ceremonies of initiation, invent mysterious codes and passwords, turn Freemason, Oddfellow, Rosicrucian, member of the Illuminati. The most successful game I ever had with two of my children – and we played it every night for months just before their bedtime – was based on their remembering a monstrous rigmarole of questions and answers, which they often recollected when I forgot, that admitted them to some secret order we had cooked up between us. Their eyes immense, solemn, shining, they stood before me, night after night, motionless and quiet but poised on the edge of abandon – for if the ritual broke down anywhere they would throw themselves about and scream with laughter – and go through the maze of nonsense we had devised. This was how the day should end, and they were sharply disappointed if I happened to be engaged elsewhere; for they could not play this game by themselves, and their mother, like any sensible woman, would have no truck with such solemn piffle, meant only for men and small children. Their delight brought me mine. But I have never felt that I could play such games – though they are common enough – with a lot of other heavy middle-aged men, all wearing fancy dress and spectacles.

42

Mineral water in bedrooms of foreign hotels

Drinking mineral water in the bedrooms of foreign hotels. Especially in France and Italy, where I eat far too much, take more wine than agrees with me, and so soon exist in a surfeited liverish condition, am yawny, headachy, and in a torment of thirst. How delightful then to escape from the cathedrals and art galleries, the laborious encounters with distinguished foreign colleagues, to take off one's coat and shoes in the plushy hermitage of the bedroom, and to receive from the waiter a bottle, fresh off the ice, of whatever brand of *eau minérale* they fancy round there! It will have been awarded gold medals and diplomas. It will attempt to cure rheumatism, catarrh of the stomach, urinary complaints, obesity and gout, gravel and stone. It is recommended by doctors who look like

Daudet and Zola characters. But not only is it good, this mineral water (any brand), it is also beautiful. It gurgles out of its green bottle like a chill and sparkling mountain spring, and arrives in the furred desert of my throat like a benediction; and as I sit there, in my shirt-sleeves and socks, swilling it down, knowing that rheumatism, catarrh of the stomach, urinary complaints, obesity and gout, gravel and stone are now being sharply challenged, I forgive my fellowmen, no matter how bearded and incomprehensible, and think much better of myself and of life in this world.

43

Coming of the idea

The coming of the *Idea*. There is nothing piecemeal about its arrival. It comes as the ancient gods and goddesses must have manifested themselves to their more fortunate worshippers. (And indeed it comes from the same place.) At one moment the mind knows it not. The next moment it is there, taking full possession of the mind, which quivers in ecstatic surrender. I have been accused – and not unjustly – of having too many ideas. "More hard work, more patience," they tell me, "and not so many ideas, my boy." But although hard work and patience may bring rewards I shall never know, where is the ravishing delight in them? Lord, let me live to welcome again with all the old abandon, not knowing whether I am dressing or undressing, whether it is Tuesday morning or Friday evening, the sunburst of the Idea!

44

Stereoscope

Re-discovering the stereoscope. You soon get tired of the thing, of course, but then if you leave it alone for a few years and then re-discover it, the old queer magic begins working again. Nothing that we have invented since the stereoscope, an old toy by this time, has to my mind offered us an adequate substitute for its peculiar enchantment. Its secret is that, having attained at last the third dimension, it begins to remind us of the fourth dimension, that of Time. When it is working well, the stereoscope offers us a sudden halt along the fourth dimension. Time's express unexpectedly comes to a standstill. Through its eyepieces we catch a glimpse of a moment frozen for ever. A little conjuring trick with space turns into a trick with Time. Probably the best description of the stereoscopic effect is in Rupert Brooke's "Dining-room Tea":

I saw the marble cup; the tea,
Hung on the air, an amber stream;

Stereoscope

I saw the fire's unglittering gleam,
The painted flame, the frozen smoke.
No more the flooding lamplight broke
On flying eyes and lips and hair;
But lay, but slept unbroken there,
On stiller flesh, and body breathless,
And lips and laughter stayed and deathless,
And words on which no silence grew.

That – and pretty good writing too, much better than anything Brooke's critics offer us – is dining-room tea as seen through the stereoscope. There are industrious amateurs of the camera who make their own stereoscope views, and no doubt many of them have old moments of family history preserved in this fashion. To me they would be unbearable, altogether too poignant. No movement, not a flicker, no reaching toward us; but there, clear and smiling in the sunlight, the dead would stand, youth and hope would bloom again, and the very rose bushes and patches of lawn would rend the heart. The stereoscopic views that I possess, and in which I find delight, have nothing to do with me; and in them it is not my own bit of Time, but the world's, which stands still. And sometimes with a rum ironic effect too. I found an old batch of these views during the war. One of them, perhaps fifty years old, was particularly charming. In it was a high summer in the Bavarian Alps: a steep path descended to a broad village street, and an old peasant woman pulled a small cart up this path; and, looking over a wooden railing in the foreground, were a youngish man in Bavarian peasant costume, who was smoking a pipe, and a buxom woman also in peasant costume; and down below, across the street, were tall houses with steep roofs and pointed towers, and beyond were thick woods and the foothills, and beyond them the mountains powdered with snow, and the sharp tooth of the Watzmann. It was an idyllic scene. I felt I would give a good deal, especially after several years of bombed London and the black-out, to saunter down this path, exchange a word with the man with the long pipe, and then stroll on the sunny side of the street below. The description on the back of the stereograph began enthusiastically: "This is one of the most famous mountain resorts in the German Alps. You can find few spots even in Switzerland with scenery as grand ... there are endless possibilities in the way of walking and mountain climbing...." And the name of this delightful place was Berchtesgaden. But in that captured moment of its time, not even the faintest shadow of a swastika mars the sunlight, and Hitler is still a queer sulky lad over in Austria. Perhaps once he saw this same stereoscopic view, saw the same steep path, the two peasants, the old woman and her cart, the fairy-tale roofs and towers among the woods; and it is possible that it was some such glimpse that began it all – he would find his way into this scene, accompanied perhaps by Wagnerian strings and trombones, even if in the end he had to wade through blood into it. To think they are all there, Hitler, Goering, Goebbels, Himmler, all the black brutes of the S.S. waiting to enter this scene at their appointed place along the time track!

45

Seeing the actors

When I was a lad and regularly took my place in the queue for the early doors of the gallery in the old Theatre Royal, Bradford, the actors on their way to the stage door had to walk past us. I observed them with delight. In those days, actors looked like actors and like nothing else on earth. There was no mistaking them for wool merchants, shipping clerks, and deacons of Baptist chapels, all those familiar figures of my boyhood. They wore suits of startling check pattern, outrageous ties, and preposterous overcoats reaching down to their ankles; They never seemed to remove all their make-up as actors do now, and always had a rim of blue-black round their eyelids. They did not belong to our world and never for a moment pretended to belong to it. They swept past us, fantastically overcoated, with trilbies perched raffishly on brilliantined curls, talking of incredible matters in high tones, merely casting a few sparkling glances – all the more sparkling because of that blue-black – in our direction; and then vanished through the stage door, to reappear, but out of all recognition, in the wigs and knee-breeches of *David Garrick* or *The Only Way*. And my young heart, as innocent as an egg, went out to these romantic beings; and perhaps it was then, although I have no recollection of it, that the desire was born in me to write one day for the Theatre. Now, after working on so many stages, I know all about actors, and I doubt if the very least of their innumerable maddening tricks and absurd egoisms has escaped my observation; but, quite apart from the work we do together and without reference to the needs of my profession, I have a soft spot for actors, and probably it is because of that old delight I used to feel as they went swaggering past us on their way to the stage door. And indeed I sometimes wish they would swagger more now, buy bigger overcoats and wilder hats, and retain those traces of make-up that put them outside respectability and kept them rogues and vagabonds, which is what at heart – bless 'em! – they are.

46

Sunday papers in the country

A most mysterious source of delight, arising from the unexpected arrival of Sunday newspapers in the country. When I am in London I care less than a fig whether I have the Sunday papers or not; but if I am staying deep in the country, far away from shops or any regular delivery of papers, and if by any lucky chance these papers are brought to the house, then I am as much delighted as if I had been given a fine present, exclaiming in a kind of rapture at the very sight of the *Observer*, *Sunday Times*, *Sunday Express*, *Sunday Pictorial*, and the *News of the World*. And why – I cannot imagine.

47

Long trousers

There was a time when merely wearing long trousers brought me delight. In those days, when I must have been about fifteen, I had only one suit – my best – with long trousers. My other suits had knee-breeches, buttoning tightly just below the knee and worn with thick long stockings, turned down at the top. There was really nothing wrong with my appearance when I wore these knee-breeches and long stockings, for after years of football I had muscular well-shaped legs; but whenever I wore them I felt I was still imprisoned, a shame-faced giant, in the stale miniature world of childhood. Condemned – and I use this term because there were strict rules at home about which suits could be worn – to wear these knee-breeches, I felt that no glimpse of my real self could catch the town's eye: I might almost have been sent to school in a pram. Conversely I felt that as soon as I put on the long trousers then appearance and reality were gloriously one; I joined the world of men; and even without doing anything more than wear these trousers – and leaving the other wretched things at home I could feel my whole nature expanding magnificently. On the occasional days when I was allowed to wear the adult trousers to go to school, I almost floated there. Never did eighteen inches of cloth do more for the human spirit. On those mornings now when I seem to stare sullenly at the wreck of a shining world, why do I not remind myself that although I grow old and fat and peevish *at least I am wearing my long trousers?*

48

Planning travel

Planning travel. I still find this delightful, whereas travel itself seems to me now a very dubious enterprise. But with paper and a sharp pencil and plenty of tobacco, together with a calendar and maps and time-tables in front of me, I can still recapture the old bewitchery. For an hour or two I dismiss the hours of boredom that lie in wait for me, the indigestion and incredible beds, the monstrous service charges and appeals for tips, the humiliating servitude to passport and customs officials and currency regulations, the ever wilder and more desperate packing, the soiled shirts and the socks with holes in them, the cold, the heat, the dust and flies, the headaches far from home. The maps and time-tables say nothing of these things but yet contrive to suggest dawn in the mountains, sunset in the desert, the oranges outside the window, moonrise over strange water, smiling brown faces, laughter in the night. I am no lover of air travel but I must confess that for happy Planning I would not now be without *The ABC International Airways and Shipping Guide*, which is one of the few successful poetic works of our time and might well be considered for the Nobel Prize.

49

Metaphysics

In my time I have found delight among the metaphysicians, especially those who are most ingenious in their dialectic. McTaggart, for example. I used to attend some of his more elementary lectures at Cambridge, and enjoyed every moment of them. He would stand with his head to one side, looking like a colossal pink schoolboy reciting a lesson, with a kind of owlish innocence about him; and, after many instances that would involve pink elephants or unicorns, would exile into limbo the materialists and dualists and then proceed to establish in the upper air his own crystal castle of idealism. Reading him even now, I recover some of that old delight. It is the superb technique and the smiling confidence, like those of a juggler, that give me such pleasure. I am no disciple of Professor Ayer – and have no pretensions to philosophy – but I never felt that McTaggart was really telling me anything about life, that he was busy revealing the truth. Not that I could ever discover any flaw in his argument.

What he set out to prove, he proved, so far as I was – and still am – concerned. I would never have dared to contradict a single statement he ever made. Always I floated easily with him up to that castle hanging in mid-air. But I never really believed a word of it. I came away from him, however, refreshed and enriched by the experience as if I had spent an hour with a benevolent wizard. Are they all gone now, these illusionists of logic, these verbal jugglers? Are there no undergraduates anywhere who are turned once or twice into gaping Aladdins?

50

Early childhood and the treasure

I can remember, as if it happened last week, more than half a century ago, when I must have been about four and, on fine summer mornings, would sit in a field adjoining the house. What gave me delight then was a mysterious notion, for which I could certainly not have found words, of a Treasure. It was waiting for me either in the earth, just below the buttercups and daisies, or in the golden air. I had formed no idea of what this Treasure would consist of, and nobody had ever talked to me about it. But morning after morning would be radiant with its promise. Somewhere, not far out of reach, it was waiting for me, and at any moment I might roll over and put a hand on it. I suspect now that the Treasure was Earth itself and the light and warmth of the sunbeams; yet sometimes I fancy that I have been searching for it ever since.

51

Reading in bed about foul weather

There is a peculiar delight, which I can still experience though I knew it best as a boy, in cosily reading about foul weather when equally foul weather is beating hard against the windows, when one is securely poised between the wind and rain and sleet outside and the wind and rain and sleet that leap from the page into the mind. The old romancers must have been aware of this odd little bonus of pleasure for the reader, and probably that is why so many of their narratives, to give them a friendly start, began with solitary horsemen, cloaked to the eyebrows, riding through the night on urgent business for the Duke, sustained by nothing more than an occasional and dubious *ragout* or pasty and a gulp or two of sour wine (always fetched by surly innkeepers or their scowling slatterns), on side-roads deep in mire, with wind, rain, thunder-and-lightning, sleet, hail, snow, all turned on at the full. With the windows rattling away and hailstones drumming at the paper in the fireplace, snug in bed except for one cold elbow, I have travelled thousands and thousands of mucky miles with these fellows, braving the foulest nights, together crying "Bah!"

52

Having one's fortune told

Having one's fortune told. There is a double delight here. The first – and I think less important – comes simply from being the object of another human being's serious attention. The second source of delight arises from the enlargement and romantic transformation of our personal affairs, thanks to the loose, mysterious, evocative terms of fortune-telling. We are turned at once into the heroes and heroines of immense dramas in blank verse. The scale is Homeric. The atmosphere borrows something from the Arabian Nights. We go on journeys, not to neighbouring market-towns but apparently to remote continents. We do not stay in hotels but sleep – if any sleep is to be had there – in "strange beds", perhaps lent by Haroun Al Raschid. Dark men, probably ebony-hued and nine feet high, and fair woman, so many Snow Queens or princesses out of Maeterlinck, flit through these vague but impressive narratives. We gain and lose not fifty pounds here and a hundred there, but, it seems, vast fortunes, whole caravans loaded down with rubies. The tepid routine of our existence drops out, unnoticed. Our acquaintances go roaring up into gigantic life as Dear Devoted Friends and Powerful Determined Enemies. We live for five minutes like Alexander, Caesar and Genghis Khan. So in the mild patter of the lady staring at our palms or at the cards we have cut, we catch echoes of the lost voices from our most grandiose dreams.

53

Wood

I am not as clumsy with my hands as many bookish men I know, but I have never had any training or practice in handicrafts, and apart from sawing and splitting logs and knocking a nail in here and there, I have had little to do with wood. Yet I never go where wood is being worked, never stand near a joiner, carpenter or cabinet-maker, without feeling at least a tickle of delight. To handle newly-planed wood, even to look at it or smell it, is to receive a message that life can still be in good heart. The very shavings are a crisp confirmation. There is a mystery here. Atavism will not explain it. Our remoter ancestors, winding back into the mists, were chippers of stone. I have seen their flints, inside and outside museums, and have never yet felt a quiver of sympathy. Woodwork as we know it, needing sharp metal tools, must be one of man's newer activities. Is this perhaps the secret? Is this stuff still so excitingly new? But light alloys and plastics are newer still, the discoveries of today, and yet no message comes from them. Is it because wood, no matter how chopped and trimmed and planed, somehow remains alive? I put my hand on the desk on which I am writing now, and it is almost as if my palm fell on the shoulder of a brother. Into this patient material have passed rain and sun, steely mornings in March, the glow of October: it has lived as some secret part of us still lives. And notice how few men who work with wood seem unhappy, defeated. When we write a book about a Carpenter, we call it the New Testament.

54

Comic characters

When I was a child there were fantastic comic characters about, and I delighted in them. Some of them were relatives or old friends of the family. They were as grotesque as characters out of Dickens or Gogol. They seemed to realise, like the grand drolls they were, that much was expected of them, and so they lived tremendously up to themselves, piling it on like comedians in the third act. Every time they popped up, they were better than ever. As if they *knew*. And now of course they are all long dead and gone. They were thinning out by the time the First World War arrived, and when I came back from that war the last of them had joined the dinosaurs and mastodons. Even after making all allowance for adult taste, I cannot find their like now, so all that keen delight has gone too. Yet now and again, when people come here or I go and stay somewhere, I notice that the children are behaving curiously. There are glances and nudges, watery eyes, suppressed giggles in corners, explosions on distant landings; and so it occurs to me that the delight I once knew has not entirely vanished; that some of my friends do not cut the same figure in all eyes that they do in mine; that even I myself, a worried, almost desperate man, old and solemn enough to take the Assizes, may have turned without knowing it into one of these same huge daft drolls....

55

Money for nothing

In the early nineteen-twenties, when I first settled in London, I did a great deal of reviewing. (There was much more space then for book reviews than there is now.) I was ready to review anything, and often did columns of short notes on new books. The books themselves were then sold – fiction for a third of the publisher's price, non-fiction for about a half – to a certain shop not far from the Strand, a shop that specialised in the purchase and re-sale of review copies, a traffic that had a faintly piratical air. At this shop, where human nature was understood, one was always paid at once and paid in cash, generally in exquisite new pound notes. And of all the money I have ever handled, this gave me most delight. Money for Jam, Money for Old Rope, Money for nothing. When we receive our wages, salaries or fees, we may be content, for this is what we have earned, but we are a long way from delight. It is money that we have not earned, the windfall, the magical bonus, that starts us capering. Many sociologists, who understand everything except their fellow creatures, are bewildered and saddened by the ubiquitous passion among the mob for betting and gambling. But the more we standardise wages, hours and prices, the more we insist upon social security for everybody, the more we compel two and two to make four everywhere, the more people will take to the greyhound tracks and the football pools. For it is when two and two miraculously make five that the heart leaps up at last. It is when money looks like manna that we truly delight in it. Since those days when I used to sell my review copies I have earned in one way and another very considerable sums of money indeed; but they have all been lost in a dreary maze of bank accounts, stocks and shares, tax certificates, cheques and bills and receipts. I have never felt rich and careless, like a man returning from a lucky day at the races or a sailor home from a long voyage. But when I used to hurry out of that shop with five or six new pound notes singing in my pocket, for quarter of an hour or so I felt like a tipsy millionaire or the man who broke the bank at Monte Carlo. Money to Burn! And the only comparable moments I have known since have been on certain very rare occasions when I happen to have been fortunate in playing those fruit machines, which were so popular in the American south-west when we were there. These machines are so rigged that the odds are monstrously against the customer. Nickels and quarters by the score could vanish as lemons tried to mate with plums. But the jackpot, which must surely have been the invention of some poet, more than compensated for all these losses. As the magic combination of symbols showed itself, the machine would first hesitate, then shiver and noisily gather its works together, and then, like an exasperated fairy godmother, would splutteringly hurl whole handfuls of coin at you so that below your waist it seemed to be raining nickels or quarters. This is acquisition lit with wonder and glory. We could do with more of it.

56

Children's games

If I had the sensible habit of cutting out and filing away items in the Press that seemed to me of some value, I would now have before me a letter to *The Times* about the recent disappearance of children's games. As it is, this letter exists only sketchily in my memory. But I remember that the writer – a wise man – pointed out that the games that children organise among themselves, many of them games that must have been played for centuries, are now fast vanishing; and he gave it as his opinion that this disappearance was only further evidence of a decline in real living values. Whether he was right or wrong – and I suspect he was right – it is certain that much of the delight I recollect from my earlier boyhood was associated with these games. Living on the edge of the town, in a half-built suburb, we were fortunate in our conditions; and I remember that, in spite of occasional watchmen, we made lively use of half-built houses and those triangular-shaped stacks of builders' timber that were so familiar then. The games themselves were all traditional, part of a world closed to adults. The favourites were *Tin Can Squat*, *Rally-ho*, *Duckstone*, and *Piggy*, these being the names we knew them by in our part of the West Riding. In *Tin Can Squat* (and I am spelling this last word at a venture) a small circle was marked on the ground, and a boy kicked an old tin can as far as he could out of this circle; and then, while the boy who was "it" retrieved the can and replaced it in the circle, the rest of us hid ourselves. The wretched "it", who had a hard life in this game, not only had to find one of us and declare who we were but also had to get back to the circle before somebody else dashed out from cover and kicked the can away again. This sounds pretty hopeless, but an experienced "it" who could run and knew some strategy was usually able fairly soon to put somebody else in his place. *Rally-ho* was our local term for the fine old game of Prisoners' Base, and we played it for hours at a time, well into the dusk, always with vigour and often with passion, in an atmosphere like that of some bitter Saga. I have forgotten the rules of *Duckstone* but I know that each boy had a *Duck*, which was a flattish stone, and that the boy who was "it" put his *Duck* on top of a small pile of stones while the rest of us aimed at it with our *Ducks*. He had to replace his *Duck* just as his fellow-victim had to replace the tin can, and I can still hear the triumphant cry "Your Duck's off!" And *Piggy* was the Tipcat of southern and more genteel circles. This seemed to me then – and seems to me still – a glorious game, with the simplest equipment, merely two sticks, a longish stout one to hit with and a short one, part-pointed at the ends, that was tipped up, out of its circle, and then sent whizzing as far as possible. You declared then how many running paces the *Piggy* had been knocked; and you only added these to your score if no member of the other side could reach it in fewer paces. This involved a nice calculation of distance: if you claimed too much, you added nothing to your side's score; if you were over-cautious and played safe by claiming too little, you were blamed for not adding enough to the score. It was, I repeat, a glorious game. After tipping up the *Piggy*, to catch it squarely in the middle with a full hard swing was to light a fuse of joy from the arm to the mind. And to this day I never see a short bit of stick that is narrower at each end than it is in the middle without wanting to transform it into a *Piggy*. There were other games too, such as the one in which you all jumped on a fellow's back until he guessed the number of fingers somebody held up; and they were all alike in being cheap and easy to play, though not necessarily easy to play well, and being traditional, enduring throughout the centuries in the rough-and-tumble boys' world. And now we are told that they are going – or have gone. Perhaps when our civilisation is a ruin, when there is no more radio, no more electricity for the films, the children will come running out of the shacks and dugouts to find delight again in their own games.

57

Suddenly doing nothing

Doing nothing when one ought to be doing everything. It must not be confused with simply doing nothing at any time, which is mere sloth. In order to know this particular delight, you have to be a busy chap, preferably concerned in a number of different enterprises. If they are important and apt to develop dramatically, so much the better. A few worrying colleagues, with a passion for long-distance telephoning, cables and telegrams, will add spice to the dish. Now let these various enterprises be brought nearly to the boil. You have spent at least several days rushing from one to the other, explaining everywhere how desperately busy you are, with one eighteen-hour day after another, secretaries fainting, wife telephoning to the doctor about you; no time to eat properly, just living on brandy and mysterious blue capsules. Then, slap in the middle of all this hullabaloo, pack it up for a day or two, allowing each gang to conclude you are toiling for one of the other gangs, and do nothing, absolutely nothing. Eat and drink and smoke, of course; yawn and stretch and scratch; glance at newspapers, dip into light literature, and gossip; but no more. No gardening, sharp walks, correspondence, nor even jobs about the house. Get as close to doing nothing as it is possible for a Western Aryan or whoever we are. Give an occasional thought, for spice and devilment, to the worrying colleagues. Refuse to answer the telephone - too busy. It is a dirty trick – but delicious.

58

Pleasure and gratitude of children

I doubt if there is anything in my life that I regret more bitterly than I do my frequent failure as a boy to bring delight to my parents by showing them how pleased I was. Time after time, I realise now, I must have brought them bewilderment, dismay, and aching disappointment, by failing to respond adequately to some treat they planned for me. When, for example, they took me to London and to the Franco-British Exhibition. What a misery I must have been! There has always been in me a little devil – or, if you prefer it, a perverse rather than boorish streak – that will not allow me to show pleasure when it is expected of me. The moment of unwrapping the present, of responding to congratulations, of seeing at last what has been so lovingly planned and carried out for me, always finds me staring out of a pewter-coloured eye, frowning, hesitant, mumbling, blankly unappreciative. I can light up at some unexpected bit of nonsense, often at the smallest attention, but at the appointed and long-expected hour, when the least quiver on my face is of some significance, I flop heavily. And the worst victims of any such inadequacy or perversion are parents. I know that now, being a parent myself, although my children are far more responsive than I ever was. I understand now how easily I could have delighted my own parents. For to show a child what has once delighted you, to find the child's delight added to your own, so that there is now a double delight seen in the glow of trust and affection, this is happiness. I would rather see one of my children's faces kindle at the sight of the quay at Calais than be offered the chance of exploring by myself the palaces of Peking. How good it is to recapture old and fast-fading delights, to see them anew through love, and to find them sparkling and glowing now like jewels!

59

Atmosphere of billiards

Years ago I made up my mind that as soon as I had a house with sufficient space in it, I would have a billiard room. I do not play billiards very well, and play snooker rather worse; but I delight in these games, especially under my own roof. This is partly an affair of atmosphere. Billiards does not, in my mind, belong to the strictly contemporary world of split atoms and splitting personalities. It belongs to a smaller, cosier and far more secure world, rooted somewhere in the 'Nineties. Possibly the reason why I feel this is that when I was very young and slept in the front attic, I used to take from the back attic, which was our lumber room, many copies of an illustrated weekly called *Today*. This weekly, defunct when I read it, was edited by Jerome K. Jerome and appeared, I fancy, in the earlier 'Nineties. Among its features was a series of drawings known as *Humours of the Billiard*

Room or something of the sort, drawings filled with moustached, shirt-sleeved gents grappling with the jigger among the fumes of hot toddy and tuppenny cigars. This atmosphere of the more bourgeois 'Nineties at play still haunts the game for me. So when I switch on the six lights and the green cloth leaps into its own Maytime, when I take off my coat and chalk my cue, something of the cosy security of childhood returns to me, aircraft and radio have not yet been invented, torture is unheard-of, and Rutherford and the atom have not met. Our simplest pleasures are rarely simple, for are we not spirits, lost and probably far from home?

60

Knowing a poet

The first poet I ever met really looked the part; and although that was nearly forty years ago and I have met scores and scores of poets since, I think he looked the part better than any of his successors. He was shaggy and leonine, with formidable brows above deep-set eyes and hollowed cheeks. If he read his work – and he took no persuading – he intoned it in the grand manner, with his eyes flashing away and one hand beating the measure. He did not live in a world of typewriters and agents and contracts with the B.B.C. He was published, it is true, and would sometimes refer with gratitude or scorn to reviews of his work. But this was merely an occasional descent from some prophetic height. He seemed to cohabit with the Sublime. He was not a chap who wrote verse, but the Bard. He could trumpet with laughter, but like so many romantic persons, who have a kind of innocence about them, he had no sense of humour, and probably was better without it. He was no fool, except in the sense in which all really nice people are fools, and was often shrewd in his judgments of both persons and issues; but his outlook, from his invisible mountain top, was magnificently poetical. If he did not actually wear a cloak, he seemed to do, above his astonishingly hairy tweeds; and somehow his hats hinted at Merlin. His family and friends loved him, and so did I. And as a youth, encountering the Idea made manifest, I delighted in him.

61

Giving advice

Giving advice, especially when I am in no position to give it and hardly know what I am talking about. I manage my own affairs with as much care and steady attention and skill as - let us say - a drunken Irish tenor. I swing violently from enthusiasm to disgust. I change policies as a woman changes hats. I am here today and gone tomorrow. When I am doing one job, I wish I were doing another. I base my judgments on anything – or nothing. I have never the least notion what I shall be doing or where I shall be in six months' time. Instead of holding one thing steadily, I try to juggle with six. I cannot plan, and if I could I would never stick to the plan. I am a pessimist in the morning and an optimist at night, am defeated on Tuesday and insufferably victorious by Friday. But because I am heavy, have a deep voice and smoke a pipe, few people realise that I am a flibbertigibbet on a weathercock. So my advice is asked. And then, for ten minutes or so, I can make Polonius look a trifler. I settle deep in my chair, two hundred pounds of portentousness, and with some first-rate character touches in the voice and business with pipe, I begin: "Well, I must say that in your place –" And inside I am bubbling with delight.

62

Delight in writing

I will put this in to answer a question, as yet unspoken but, I imagine, inevitable. The practised and professional writer finds little delight in writing. Most delight only comes when we are young and beginning to write and happen to find ourselves fluent, and then, while we are still highly conscious of ourselves as writers, we delight in the thought of ourselves at work writing. But later, after years of experience, so it seems to me, either we are struggling with our particular medium, making an effort that may bring its own satisfactions, but not delight; or we may find ourselves working at the highest creative pitch, and then, being possessed by what we are doing, there is not room in us for any feeling of delight. The older writer, I think, discovers most pleasure at the beginning and end of a piece of work; first, in accepting the idea and then envisaging its possibilities; last, in returning to the completed work and trying to bring it nearer to perfection, at which task, though I claim delight for it here, I am no great shakes.

63

Not going

One of the delights known to age and beyond the grasp of youth is that of *Not Going*. When we are young it is almost agony not to go. We feel we are being left out of life, that the whole wonderful procession is sweeping by, probably for ever, while we are weeping or sulking behind bars. Not to have an invitation – for the dance, the party, the match, the picnic, the excursion, the gang on holiday – is to be diminished, perhaps kept at midget's height for years. To have an invitation and then not to be able to go – oh cursed spite! Thus we torment ourselves in the April of our time. Now in my early November not only do I not care the rottenest fig whether I receive an invitation or not, but after having carelessly accepted the invitation I can find delight in knowing that I am *Not Going*. I arrived at this by two stages. At the first, after years of illusion, I finally decided I was missing nothing by not going. Now, at the second and, I hope, final stage, I stay away and no longer care whether I am missing anything or not. But don't I like to enjoy myself? On the contrary, by Not Going, that is just what I am trying to do.

64

Quietly malicious chairmanship

Quietly malicious chairmanship. There is no sound excuse for this. It is deeply anti-social, and a sudden excess of it would tear great holes in our communal life. But a man can be asked once too often to act as chairman, and to such a man, despairing of his weakness and feeling a thousand miles from any delight, I can suggest a few devices. In introducing one or two of the chief speakers, grossly over-praise them but put no warmth into your voice, only a metallic flavour of irony. If you know what a speaker's main point is to be, then make it neatly in presenting him to the audience. During some tremendous peroration, which the chap has been working at for days, either begin whispering and passing notes to other speakers or give the appearance of falling asleep in spite of much effort to keep awake. If the funny man takes possession of the meeting and brings out the old jokes, either look melancholy or raise your eyebrows as high as they will go. Announce the fellow with the weak delivery in your loudest and clearest tones. For any timid speaker, officiously clear a space bang in the middle and offer him water, paper, pencil, a watch, anything. With noisy cheeky chaps on their feet, bustle about the platform, and if necessary give a mysterious little note to some member of the audience. If a man insists upon speaking from the floor of the hall, ask him for his name, pretend to be rather deaf, and then finally announce his name with a marked air of surprise. After that you can have some trouble with a cigarette lighter and then take it to pieces. When they all go on and on, make no further pretence of paying any attention and settle down to drawing outrageous caricatures of the others on the platform, and then at last ask some man you particularly dislike to take over the chair, and stalk out, being careful to leave all your papers behind. And if all this fails to bring you any delight, it should at least help to protect you against further bouts of chairmanship.

65

Secret Brotherhoods

I delight in Members of the Secret Brotherhood. This requires some explanation. Romantic dabblers in the occult are fond of telling us that there exist in the world various secret brotherhoods, descended perhaps from esoteric priesthoods of antiquity, and that the members of these mysterious organisations are obscure citizens whose real character is only known to their fellow initiates. The fate of empires and the future of whole continents are being quietly decided by a little solicitor from Newport, Monmouth, a market-gardener in Lanark, a dealer in picture-frames from Montparnasse, and an insurance broker in Trieste. A leather merchant from Belgrade has a compartment on the Orient Express, and into this compartment a Viennese oboe player introduces an importer of oriental curios from Cairo – all three of them commonplace-looking middle-aged men; and after half an hour's talk the relations between Europe and Africa are settled for the next ten years; and a message is sent to the Deputy Grand Master, who keeps a pawnshop in Cape Town. I do not believe this. From an author's point of view it is too good to be true. But if there were such secret brotherhoods, then most of us have occasionally met the kind of men who ought to be members of them. They are men who give us the impression that they have deliberately turned aside from power and fame. They are content to be comparatively obscure, to be known only to a small circle of friends and acquaintances, who do not hesitate to turn to them for guidance and help at times of crisis. They are not failures, except in the eyes of the vulgar and stupid. They may not be mystics, though I doubt if any of them are ever found with a materialist philosophy, but, like the mystics, their lives appear to be rooted in some other world. They earn a living but never join in the general grab for prizes, possessions, fat jobs and bouquets. Except when their help is urgently demanded, they are never quite with us. They are friendly but never babblingly intimate. From the standpoint of "Who's Who" and Fleet Street, they are nonentities; but in the circles where they are known, they are deeply respected and have much influence. We feel they could have been rich, powerful, famous, if they had wanted to be; but preferred another way of life. They are leaders who do not choose to lead. On the other hand, they are never missionaries, fanatical propagandists, martyrs. They are extraordinary men pretending, fairly successfully, to be ordinary men. They appear to be having a rest in this life, or to be waiting for some signal that the bulk of us will never recognise. There are never many of them, and perhaps we meet a true specimen of the type about once every ten years. And just as I do not delight in the powerful and famous, who have been mostly ruined on the way up, so I do delight in these Members of the Secret Brotherhood, the men who have never started to climb and who seem to have looked in on us from some other and better planet.

66

Cosy with work

In our younger days we writers – or composers or painters – like to talk a lot about work and what we are going
to do, but we do not like actually working, which usually
means removing ourselves from the company of other
great souls and toiling away in solitude. This becomes
easier as we get older, and once we are well into our
professional middle-age, instead of being reluctant we are
often eager to disappear into our work and are angry
when we are prevented from toiling in solitude. Indeed, I
often feel delight now in merely surveying my desk and the
rather pitiful implements of my craft (and here the painter
has the advantage) laid out on that desk, all waiting for
me. Typewriter, paper, pencils and erasers, notebooks,
works of reference – they are all ready for me, these sensible old colleagues. Here is my own tiny world that I
understand. The other world, so vast, so idiotic, is now
shut out and can be forgotten for a few hours. And this
gives me now as much delight as I used to feel, as a young

man, when I was on my way to some party and imagined how I would astonish everybody. But although this change of outlook makes it easier to fulfil all contracts and earn a living, it has its dangers, as we can see from the dim and complacent work of so many elderly artists. It is possible to be too cosy on the job, to shut out the huge daft world too completely. This is in fact a dangerous delight, and has probably ruined more good men than booze and low company ever did.

67

Other people's weaknesses

What delight we give other people by confessing to absurd weaknesses! For example, I cannot endure being tossed about in small boats, where I sweat with terror. Again, the sight and sound of a bat or a bird fluttering and banging about in a room fill me with a disgust that can leap to fear and panic. When I have admitted this, I have seen people light up for the first time in their converse with me. At last I have succeeded in pleasing them. Until then, apparently, I have been insufferable. And I behave in the same fashion. I delight in J's terror of public speaking, in M's horror of spiders, in A's fear of being left alone in any old house, in H's rejection of all flying, in W's shuddering withdrawal from any cat. We like to feel that there is an equitable rationing system for this nonsense, and that we are all at times still children huddling together in the dark. A man or woman whose personality had not a speck of such weakness would be intolerable, not one of us at all, a sneering visitor from some other planet. Now and again they turn up, and we are delighted to see them go.

68

Bragging

Bragging. It is true, as my family have pointed out more than once (families overdo this kind of thing), that now and again I delight in bragging. But I do it, as of course I do everything, from the best of motives. When I am with people who think I am a fine fellow and have done some good work in my time, I am (or at least I imagine I am) modest, almost ready to blush, candid about my faults, humbly aware of how little I have done to merit such praise, etc., etc., etc. But there are some persons who do not appear to understand that I exist just as they and their friends exist, that what I do seems as important to me as what they do seems to them, that I have a world of my own just as they and their kind have a world of their own. They are people composed of blank stares, ignorance, incredulity and insensitiveness. In a ruder society, they would be taken out into the castle yard and banged over the head with spiked maces. In our society, this is not possible. So I assert myself, I become aggressive, I begin to brag. But I am not doing this merely for myself. I am proclaiming the existence of a whole world of wonder and glory. I am taking my stand for Literature and Drama and the author's way of life. I am glaring and shouting on behalf of Sophocles and Shakespeare, Cervantes and Molière. Mightier than the sword, Major Fawcett! Yes, and let me tell *you* something –

69

Plots

The older I get, the more I delight in plots. I am referring of course to fiction and the drama and not to real life, in which it is only politically-minded persons of the extreme Left and the extreme Right who see everywhere, in place of the drift the rest of us notice, so many closely-woven elaborate plots. One of the reasons why I read so many detective stories is that the best of them offer me highly ingenious plots, in which it is possible to find an aesthetic pleasure. And now and again I write a play that is, so far as I am concerned, although I may hint at a social purpose just to keep in the movement, simply an opportunity to enjoy myself constructing and working out to the last artful detail – a plot. Plotting is not fashionable either in fiction or the drama. The most admired novelists and dramatists of this age are anything but plotters. They wish to expose the quivering nerves of life, to show us certain moments in all their poignant vividness, to take us down among the dark springs of character and action, to alternate between lyricism and harsh prophecy. Bravo! But all this does not exhaust the possibilities of the novel and the play. There are other powers and pleasures. And one of them is this imposing of an elaborate artificial pattern upon the muddle of character and action, this contriving of a much smaller but infinitely neater and more logical world out of the far larger and messier one. Old-fashioned? At the moment – and then only in tiny critical circles – certainly. But this distaste for plots is nothing but a passing fad of criticism. Plotting, take my word for it, will come back soon, probably with a rush. And if I were a young novelist I would begin to plot, preferably on a large scale, stamping a pattern of immediate cause and effect, so many wheels and chains, on the putty of our post-war urban society. To work, my boys – cheerily now!

70

Being solemn about one's tastes

Like you, I am always delighted to declare my tastes, prejudices, preferences. And probably like you too, I hide this delight behind an appearance of awful solemnity. I never look graver and more weighty than at these moments. "No," I say, as if sentencing somebody to death, "I don't care for fried tomatoes." And I give one of my listeners a searching look, then stare severely at any object in the middle distance, and sit there, mute, heavy, rigid, practically a tablet of stone. Or I hold up a hand that apparently weighs about a hundred and fifty pounds, command silence, and then announce in a massive tone: "If I'm hot – give me a shower every time." Sometimes, together with the air of finality that is always there, you will catch a slow sad rhythm, as if a humanitarian prime minister were declaring war: "No, I can't smoke a Light Virginian flake. It burns my tongue." And there are times when beneath the grave weighty manner are abysses of bitter-ness, unfathomable depths of despair, as if all life on this planet had been a blunder: "Oh, do you?" I cry, seeming to glare at them out of bloody sockets. "I much prefer the old-fashioned folding ones. Only of course they're so hard to find now."

71

Dreams

Dreams. Now and again I have had horrible dreams, but not enough of them to make me lose my delight in dreams. To begin with, I like the idea of dreaming, of going to bed and lying still and then, by some queer magic, wandering into another kind of existence. As a child I could never understand why grown-ups took dreaming so calmly when they could make such a fuss about any holiday. This still puzzles me. I am mystified by people who say they never dream and appear to have no interest in the subject. It is much more astonishing than if they said they never went out for a walk. Most people – or at least most Western Europeans – do not seem to accept dreaming as part of their lives. They appear to see it as an irritating little habit, like sneezing or yawning. I have never understood this. My dream life does not seem as important as my waking life, if only because there is far less of it, but to me it is important. As if there were at least two extra continents added to the world, and lightning excursions running to them at any moment between midnight and breakfast. Then again, the dream life, though queer and bewildering and unsatisfactory in many respects, has its own advantages. The dead are there, smiling and talking. The past is there, sometimes all broken and confused but occasionally as fresh as a daisy. And perhaps, as Mr. Dunne tells us, the future is there too, winking at us. This dream life is often overshadowed by huge mysterious anxieties, with luggage that cannot be packed and trains that refuse to be caught; and both persons and scenes there are not as dependable and solid as they are in waking life, so that Brown and Smith merge into one person while Robinson splits into two, and there are thick woods outside the bathroom door and the dining-room is somehow part of a theatre balcony; and there are moments of desolation or terror in the dream world that are worse than anything we have known under the sun. Yet this other life has its interests, its gaieties, its satisfactions, and, at certain rare intervals, a serene glow or a sudden ecstasy, like glimpses of another form of existence altogether, that we cannot match with open eyes. Daft or wise, terrible or exquisite, it is a further helping of experience, a bonus after dark, another slice of life cut differently for which, it seems to me, we are never sufficiently grateful. Only a dream! Why *only*? It was there, and you had it. "If there were dreams to sell," Beddoes enquires, "what would you buy?" I cannot say offhand, but certainly rather more than I could afford.

72

The ironic principle

Many years ago, an old friend of my schooldays sent me an inscribed copy of a book he had written on Dairy Farming, a subject on which he was an authority. I looked at this bulky volume in despair. Clearly I could not give it away or sell it, yet nothing could have been less use to me for I cared nothing about Dairy Farming. So I pushed it away in some obscure corner of my bookshelves and then forgot about it. But now that I own a dairy herd and am breeding pedigree Guernsey stock, I need that book and I cannot find it. This is Irony at work in private life. It works equally hard in public life. Thus, at this present time, we in Britain are short of petrol and cannot run our cars as often as we should like to run them. This is partly because, in order to break the Russian blockade, we are delivering rations and coal to the people of Berlin by air, the most extravagant delivery service the world has yet known. And this policy is most warmly defended by the very people here who, four years ago, were denouncing the Berliners as sub-human creatures only fit to be exterminated. Again, to take a larger example, it is less than a hundred years ago that the Japanese, still living in a medieval dream, only asked to be left alone by Western Man. But we insisted upon their opening their ports to us, with the result that after a turn or two of the wheel there arrived the disaster of Pearl Harbour and the fall of Singapore. So it goes on. The conquerors enslave the conquered, who in turn begin to shape and colour the secret dreams and the culture of their masters. The diabolical prisoners' cage is occupied first by the sadist who designed it. The Duke of Alva ends a career of legendary terror by being breast-fed. English colonels would stamp round India for years, snorting with contempt, and return home to join the Theosophical Society. In large American cities so many people are in a hurry and drive automobiles that traffic in the congested streets goes into slow motion. In England so many people want to live on the edge of the countryside that miles and miles of it disappear into the city. Both whole communities and individuals turn their back on some pitfall and hurry off to land in another, rather deeper. Just when Man thinks he can do everything, he finds himself helpless in the clutch of some unknown force. And in this ironic principle, which appears to govern so much of our lives, I find delight. Even when it comes close and hurts, the delight is still there. "The Old So-and-so!" I mutter admiringly, from that part of me which must be immortal and invulnerable.

73

Truth and fiction

Truth's determination to keep right on being stranger than fiction. For example, a newspaper has just informed me that there has been a marriage between a bride of seventy and a bridegroom of forty-three; that their romance having begun with a helping of bread-pudding (a speciality of the bride's cuisine), they have had an eight-pound bread-pudding instead of a wedding-cake; and that there would be no immediate honeymoon because the bridegroom must return to his work at the Dogs' Home. No doubt we novelists and playwrights are capable of inventing such characters and such situations, but we have allowed ourselves to be bullied out of them. We hear a sneering little voice whispering "Absurd ... overdrawn ... unconvincing ... Dickensian ..." and so out they go, these glorious extravagances. But Reality pleases itself and does not give a damn, throwing eight-pound bread-puddings about and whisking bridegrooms back into Dogs' Homes, where our sneering critics ought to be, counting out the driest biscuits.

74

Three lighthouses

From some of our windows on a clear night you can see the flashes of three lighthouses. So what? I don't know; and don't feel like arguing about it. Try some other page.

75

This small world

Discovering once again how small the world is. Clever young monkeys can jeer their heads off, but the rest of us, who know that the world is full of howling dark wildernesses and so want to feel cosy for a while, rightly persist in being delighted by this discovery. The man in the smoke-room visited the same specialist that we did. The widow we met in Egypt is the cousin of the woman at the next table. Our boys must have gone to the same school. We must have been in San Francisco about the same time. What - do you know *him*? Why, of course, they used to live next door to us. Not old *Billy* Smith? How disgusted the young are at this kind of talk, and how delighted we old codgers are! And quite right too. For we know that just beyond the curtains, shaking a little no doubt with all our triumphant cries, are night, black as the grave, and the east wind and Siberia and the Okhotsk Sea and the endless wastes of the North Pacific; that in East Asia alone are a thousand million strangers and idols with three eyes and eight arms; that half a mile from the banks of the Amazon is the jungle nobody knows, probably with spiders the size of kittens; that any small lighted place, loud with friendly talk, is almost a miracle; and that we grow old and our wounds ache and too often when we cannot sleep we remember the dead.... Why then, your brother must have been there when my uncle was there. How extraordinary! It just shows one, doesn't it, what a small place....

76

Discovering Vermeer

It was in the hot June of 1914 that, a youth of nineteen, I paid my first visit to the great gallery in Amsterdam. I went to see the Rembrandts, and I stared at them respect-fully and, when called upon to do so, made sounds suggesting wonder and admiration and joy. But nothing really happened inside me. I was at least twenty years too early. It was on that occasion, however, that I discovered Vermeer, and with him – I think for the first time – a delight in the marriage of paint to canvas. Before then, although I may have enjoyed pictures here and there, I doubt if I had ever appreciated the magic of painting. This was one of those fortunate encounters: Vermeer and I were ready for each other. I discovered at last that a paint-ing of something, anything – a brick wall, the corner of a room – could fill me with a strange joy, which might haunt me for days, if only because the artist had begun to shape and colour my own vision of things. I think I came to understand then – and I feel sure many people never understand it all their lives – that we shall do well not to look from things to pictures but from pictures to things; or, in other words, that we who are not painters should not narrowly check their vision with ours but should allow their vision to shape and colour ours. So in that June, the last of that world which had not known what war could be, odd bits of brick wall or occasional glimpses of rich-toned interiors were for me enchantingly touched up by Vermeer. And this, to say the least of it, was fun. Yes, fun. The green-gold pastures of the visual arts are so cluttered up with and trodden down by solemn donkeys, braying away, so saddled and bridled with culture that their hides are sore with it, that we are inclined to forget that these arts ought to be fun. And I never visit a gallery without wanting to cry to the sad spectators "Stop tip-toeing! Have some fun! Find some delight in this place – or march straight out!"

77

Lawn tennis

Football and cricket were the chief games of my youth, and I never started playing lawn tennis until I was past thirty. The result has been that, having no secure foundation of style, my tennis is erratic. People are always asking me about moods and inspiration in my work. But it is in my tennis that I am a creature of moods and inspiration. Try me one day and I am a rabbit. Try me another day and I am a tiger – not a tiger burning bright but a tiger of sorts. If a public opinion poll were taken on my tennis, the returns would be chaotic. I never know myself whether I shall look like Tilden or tushery. My partners are nearly always surprised, one way or the other. In my time I have slammed across services, smashes, volleys that rocked Wimbledon players, and have been carelessly slaughtered by schoolgirls. Certainly I am not a good tennis player, but on my day I might be fairly described as one of the best bad players in the world. It is on these days, which always come straight out of the blue and cannot be prepared for (so I am no tournament man), that the game yields delight. The ball suddenly becomes twice its usual size, and the opposite side of the court obligingly enlarges itself too. The racket strings hum some faint rune of victory. Time stretches out to allow easy preparation for every shot, but once the balls have crossed the net, by some friendly device of relativity, slow time changes to fast. And – at last – miraculous half-volleys come off. On such afternoons, when the very sunlight has a different quality, all winds fade away, and my trousers keep up, the game takes on a large Homeric air; all thought of the insane world beyond the court hastens out of the mind; and we are at battle and at play, immortal beings, in the Maytime of a favoured planet. "Sorry, partner!" Yes, I have muttered it ten thousand times, while seeing the green or red ground open into a chasm of disgust and self-contempt. But on my day, when in the mood, when inspiration descends upon me and my racket – what delight!

78

Not having to read books

A tiny helping, not more than a twinkle now and again, but perhaps worth noting. For years and years and years – as a schoolboy, an undergraduate, a publisher's reader, an over-worked reviewer, a critic and biographer, a member of the Selection Committee of the Book Society, a journalist and student of public affairs – I have had to read a lot of books I never wanted to read. And now at last I can please myself what I read, and it is delightful. *Piers Plowman: A Study* – no, sir. *Metternich And* – no, no. *Hidden Byways In Ancient Tuscany* and *The Charm of Ceylon* – never. *Life and Times of Lord Dreary* – keep it. *More Problems of Configuration in the Gestalt Theory* – you try them. *Aftermath of Potsdam* – cannot touch an Aftermath. *Consequences of* – no, none of them. *In the Rhythm of Blue* – certainly not. *The Case of the Vanishing Cockatoo* – certainly – delighted!

79

Homage to Moszkowski

If I pass him by, who will praise Moritz Moszkowski? The musical scholars and critics are eternally busy – and quite right too – with their Bach, Mozart, Beethoven, Wagner and Brahms. Little Moritz has no place among the great. No music of his will ever disturb or challenge the soul. Neither I nor anybody else has ever come away from a composition of his, reeling and enraptured. His symphony, his opera, his concerto and concert studies are forgotten, and, although stranger things have happened, it is unlikely that any of them will be re-discovered and reviewed. In his day he had his triumphs, but every garland has been dust these many years. Yet here and now, ignoring the giants who are always willing to take another bow, I crook my finger and, to the astonishment of the company, cry "Maestro Moszkowski, forward!" For has he not given me delight, hours and hours of it, glittering like the

Carnival at Nice and yet as innocent as a baby's birthday? And all those who, like me, have pounded away at his "From Foreign Parts" and his Spanish Dance duets, should join me in this place, clapping the hands that still seem to ache from his "Bolero", and shouting "Bravo, Moritz Moszkowski, Bravo!"

80

Locusts I have known

The years that the locust hath eaten. Quite so. But what delightful locusts I have known in my time! The music hall comics who entertained me, chiefly by their almost sublime incongruity (there was one who brought on with him a little gate and walked through it to greet us), when I ought to have been learning Commercial French and the technique of woolcombing. Ancient Mariners in pubs. Witty boozers in Fleet Street bars who took time and money I could not afford. All the actors who have kept me up far too late in Midland hotels, listening to theatrical stories. The authors of second-rate romances and incredible thrillers, which I have gobbled when I might have been tasting Milton and Henry James. Strange liars in the smoke-rooms of liners. Chaps who arrived with model theatres, patent tobacco-pipes, or astonishing theories of Time and the Universe. The Marx Brothers. The

Crazy Gang. Dear old Sir Arthur with whom I played bad tennis and even worse bridge so often when I ought to have been working. The American inventor of the card game of Oklahoma, which is superior to both the musical show and the state bearing that name. All the managers and producers with whom I have wasted days chattering about impossible casts for plays. Locusts to a man, all of you, and terrible devourers of years – but I forgive you.

81

Being recognised

Being recognised, named, and greeted by headwaiters, barmen, waiters, porters, cloakroom attendants, and lift-men. There is no more contemptible entry in these pages than this, but we are what we are – and truth will out. I will confess the delight, of small voltage and short duration; but insist upon adding that I have never bought my way into this recognition. Indeed, to prove that money is not doing it, I am inclined to be on the mean side in my tipping; but I find it hard to keep a slightly sycophantic grin off my face when the types listed above proceed to do their stuff at me. Heigh-ho!

82

First time abroad

In some magnificent June weather in 1913, before the politicians began to rule our lives from dawn until midnight and before we had to ask permission from their spies to travel, I was in a small steamer from Goole that was on its way to Copenhagen to bring back butter. The North Sea that week was as blue as any that Ulysses ever saw. I had never been so far out before, and I stood for hours at one end or other of the vessel, following the fading patterns of foam and composing bad verse. Then there came a morning when we moved no longer but tied up in the shadow of steep roofs and gables out of fairy tales. A thousand exquisite blonde girls were cycling to unimaginable destinations. Plump stevedores, smoking cigars and looking as prosperous as aldermen, took note of our existence. All was as clear and bright as a picture book, yet strange, foreign. We had arrived in Copenhagen, and for the first time in my life I was abroad. Ah – what delight!

83

Transport in films

Nobody ever mentions it – but what delights me most in the unreal world of the films is the transport in that world, so different from ours. These transport arrangements and facilities seem to me far more fascinating than the faces and figures of the female stars. Travel in the film world is so smooth, punctual, speedy and effortless. Down here on earth, where objects are both heavy and malicious, we move around with difficulty. Our cars refuse to start – or, when started, shake and bump us. Taxis are not always to be found, and, when found, often behave badly. Trains are frequently late in both arriving and departing. Once on the run, then they rattle and roar and may give us headaches. Ships mostly set sail some hours after the proper time; they smell of paint, cabbage, oilskins and bilge water; they shiver and roll and pitch; and arrive on Thursday evening instead of Tuesday morning. As for air travel, it mostly consists of long waits in sheds haunted by stale cigars or on bleak windy landing grounds. And always, by air, sea or rail, there is the misery of luggage, the malice of heavy objects. But in the phantasmagoric world of the moving pictures, cars start up at once, taxis appear promptly, and all of them glide away like gondolas; trains arrive or depart within two seconds; and no sooner has any important character wandered on to an airfield than a suitable aircraft comes roaring up, lets down its steps, whisks him or her inside, and takes off before you can say "Metro-Goldwyn-Mayer". Except in the comic films, which are closer to our world, the luggage problem does not exist, huge cabin trunks being magically projected into distant hotel suites. What these film characters say and do at the end of a journey often inspires nothing in me but a sour derision. I do not envy them their love affairs, the work they never do, the fun they are supposed to be having, their clothes and their parties, the roast sirloin and the ice pudding they order but never eat. But I delight in their transport facilities, which are such stuff as dreams are made on....

84

Streets like stage sets

There is to me a curious pleasure, sometimes leaping to delight, in coming upon a real street scene that looks like a good stage set. The older parts of London are rich in these illusions, especially on a clear early evening. You turn a corner, and there happens to be nobody about and the noise of traffic has faded and the light is falling in a theatrical fashion, and for a moment you seem to be in a theatre, waiting for the opening scene of a masterpiece. There is a bit of St. James's that I must have caught a score of times at these moments, all deserted and exquisitely lit, and I have loitered there, half expecting some Fainall or Witwoud to make a teetering entrance in full Restoration costume ...

85

Nature as last consolation

Buried deep in me, I fancy, is a tiny Wordsworth or Thoreau, crying reedily to be let out. For when I imagine all else failing me, always I see myself finding my last delight in Nature herself. We will say that the world I have known is in ruins, my work is done, my family and friends are scattered, and I am a shambling old wreck of a fellow living on four-pence; nearly the worst has happened. But Nature, I tell myself, will still be there, and at last I shall turn to her with all my heart and mind. At last I shall name that flower, name that bird. A celandine in the January grass will light up a whole morning. The sound of a stonechat will fill in and complete an afternoon. I shall totter along the hedgerows, chuckling in senile joy. I shall join a club of oaks and elms. I shall fall in love with and begin courting a spray of plum-blossom. And delight shall soar into ecstasy when a great shaft of late afternoon sunlight reaches the upper downland, bright against a sky of pewter, and my rheumy eyes seem to stare at the fields of Paradise. Patience, patience, my minikin Wordsworth, my foetal Thoreau: your turn will come.

86

China and the Chinese

I have never been to China, and I suspect that if I did go there I should dislike the place. Probably I should find it far too big, with far too many people in it, a huge wilderness of alien faces, noises and smells. But all my days I have delighted in those glimpses I have caught of the Celestial Empire through the tiny windows of its paintings, drawings, pottery, poems and wise anecdotes. And I do not want an up-to-date China on either the American or Russian plan. The world seems so much poorer now that the fantastic old Empire has gone like smoke – all the poetical civil servants, the philosophical generals, the unimaginable emperors and their golden girls – and now that there is merely another vast Asiatic country filled with people clamouring for cigarettes and canned goods. When I read of "The Festival of Purity and Brightness" and the almond trees in blossom and the willows a tender green in the rain, there is delight in my heart; but any news of the Chinese Trades Union Congress will leave me as it found me. So I must return to those tiny windows, through which thousands of years of noisy swarming life have shrunk to one delicate budding branch, a river in the silver rain, one slit-eyed sage fathoms deep in meditation, a slender nameless girl, a fish or a bird or a mulberry leaf, a cup of wine under the moon....

87

Preparing for old age

I may never reach old age, of course, but if I fail now, then it will be a thousand pities, because already in secret I am delightedly preparing to play my part as a ripe and rum old character. I must aim at just the right amount of deafness, enabling me to ignore all silly remarks and interruptions and warnings. I am beginning to lay in a stock of outrageous garments. I must practise an old lion's sudden glare and roar. But this is not enough, for I do not propose simply to be a frightening old man, a monotonous part that might soon lack an audience. No, no, I shall have my moods. Now and again my elaborate courtesy and the sweetness of my smile – and this will take some rehearsing – will astonish and overwhelm the caller. Already I have opinions and prejudices to fit out a dozen old men, but I must increase my store of anecdotes and tidy them up from time to time. And I must begin lying –

to establish the correct tone and to find an easy manner. I might make a start with Conrad, on whom I never set eyes – just a reminiscence or two; and then gradually work in Hardy, Kitchener, Crippen, Edward the Seventh, assorted Gaiety Girls. And travel too – India, China, the Gold Coast, the Marquesas in the dear old days. If the youngsters yawn in my face, I will have at them with one of my twenty scandalous remarks, which I ought to be preparing, trying out and testing, almost any time now.

88

Moments in the morning

There are mornings even now when I arrive in my study like a demi-god who has been given a planet to play with. Outside my high windows the sunlight falls lovingly on all green and growing things. The paper on my desk looks as if it could be conjured almost without effort into a masterpiece. The keyboard of the typewriter glitters invitingly. The old tin box of paper fasteners, which somehow has survived all moves and changes, looks like some battered faithful sergeant who has been at my side in a hundred battles and sieges. The work, when we get down to it, will be wonderful. And brighter than the gilt along the bookshelves are the illusions of the moment ... critics are kind and wise ... readers and audiences are enchanted.... Income tax is sixpence in the pound ... the United Nations consists of united nations ... and high and shining in the regard of all good folk everywhere is that sagacious, witty, tender, profound writer ... who, now waking from his day dream, sits down, a fat grumpy fellow, to slog away until lunchtime.

89

Orchestras tuning up

We are told that some Oriental visitor, attending one of our symphony concerts for the first time, was particularly delighted by what he thought was the opening piece on the programme, the sound of the orchestra tuning up. But I am not sure that he was wrong. *Is* there in fact anything more delightful in all the symphonies, concertos and tone-poems that follow than this anonymous opening piece, so enormous in its promise, so cunningly anticipatory of the best of what is to come. What else that we hear during the evening takes such a hold on the imagination? It is, if you like, a chaos, this tuning-up-and-trying-the-instrument-and-having-a-go-at-the-difficult-bit noise; but it is a chaos caught at the supreme moment, immediately before Creation. Everything of order and beauty shortly to be revealed is already there in it. Moreover, it never fails us, unlike some of the compositions that will follow it. We never find ourselves groaning over its interminable slow movements, its tedious crescendos. It is never pretentious, never bogus. It is as delightful, crammed with as much promise, the hundredth time we hear it as it was the first; and indeed I think it grows on us. Moreover, it belongs to all schools, smiling at old Haydn and yet nodding to Schönberg, and so is always in fashion. All the instruments, from the piccolo to the contra-bassoon, play their part in it. And it conducts itself and asks for no applause. Is there a good gramophone record of it? If so, my birthday is the 13th of September.

90

Dancing

Not long ago we had to entertain a party of a dozen young people, and at their request we took them to a smallish fashionable restaurant where they could dance. I was commanded to stay for an hour or so, after which I could leave the youngsters to enjoy themselves. And grumbling, I obeyed. But after a few dances, first undertaken as a duty, it would have needed a couple of policemen to drag me away from that crowded little floor. Sweating and grunting, a mad Old Man of the Tribe, I swept girls of all sizes through all manner of dances, some of which were quite new to me. I was still hard at it when the lads of the party, children of a decadent age, were missing every other dance and cooling themselves with lager. I had never been to the place before, and I have never returned to it since; but while I was there and the alternating bands kept up their rhythm, I danced my head off. And delighted in it. I cannot understand why I have not done more dancing. Except for a short period in the late 'Twenties, when we often used a large drawing-room for improvised dances with a group of neighbours, I have never done any regular dancing. Nine times out of ten, when I have danced, it is because I have found it difficult to refuse. (I am not including here the fancy stuff in far-away places, where I will try anything from a Highland reel to a Georgian *pas seul*.) I do not know why I should be reluctant to dance. It is not because I consider myself a bad dancer. As middle-aged writers go, I am a good dancer. My sense of rhythm is excellent, and I am one of those heavy chaps who are yet light on their feet – an admirable type. But although I never want to go to any place where there is dancing, and even when bullied and hustled into such a place, I hesitate to begin, once I am launched on the dance floor I go on and on, and, if the music pleases me, am lost in delight. And as long as my partner moves easily, I do not care who she is. My close relationship is really with the music and not with my partner.

In most novels, I have observed, dancing is regarded as an activity charged with sex, almost a form of making love; so that the characters of fiction have only to take a turn or two round the floor to be shaking with passion. And clearly this is how many of our moralists, too indignant to be perspicacious, regard the dancing that they denounce. But although this pastime has its roots in our erotic earth, it has never seemed to me a narrowly sexual activity at all. Dancing, I feel, restores us to the unlocalised sex of our early youth. We are moving in a faintly erotic atmosphere but seem quite free of passion ourselves. We may be dancing to the moans of the lovelorn but we are not lovelorn. It is to the rhythm that we delightedly bind our bodies. We achieve a symbiosis with a drum. And the sharp edge of consciousness is blurred, a backdoor is opened into the old forest, and we are no longer painfully ourselves, fixed in our time, but part of a long receding line of leaping and whirling folk, who enable us to blunt the sting of thought, to forget the ticking of the clock. Dancing, we are all Cinderellas at the Ball.

91

Escaping from time

There is mild delight merely in escaping from our new servitude to Time. A good holiday is one spent among people whose notions of Time are vaguer than yours. Farm workers are better-tempered than factory workers, partly because on a farm you are not bullied by clocks. Our forefathers never seem to have bothered about minutes at all, and probably did not know that hours could be so scrupulously subdivided. Coaches were advertised to leave in the early morning, at noon or at sunset, large sensible times. Then came the railways, with their 8.52 and 3.26, compelling passengers to be conscious of minutes. And now we have to think in terms of seconds or fractions of seconds – and so far no good has come of it. In the Theatre, which has kept to the comfortable old system, performances may begin roughly at seven or eight o'clock, and a minute or two do not matter, and everybody is happy. In Radio there is an endless and idiotic fuss about seconds, as if its mob of customers could not wait a single tick, and nobody is happy. The society of split seconds is also the society of split minds; and for every hundred new electric clocks, up goes another mental home. So if you would wander in search of delight, make a start by moving towards vaguer time-keeping, steering in the direction of the clockless Hesperides.

92

Bass voices

For delight in singing I ask first – and always have done – for a great rich bass. It may lack the tunefulness and flexibility of the other voices, but it has the unique advantage, to my mind, of being at once prodigious, warmly human and *real*. The great bass is not a strange musical instrument but a real man singing. I never quite believe in tenors. A bad tenor voice is idiotic; a goodish one is faintly silly; and even an exquisite one, with a Neapolitan midnight throbbing in it, has still something slightly daft and unreal about it. Among the women, the creamy mezzo-soprano has most chance of pleasing me. The *coloratura* soprano never sounds to me remotely like a human being at all, more like some giant bird, crying of joys and sorrows quite strange to me. The contralto is human enough, but seems to belong to the wrong kind of humanity for me, all anxious, solemn, priggish, doomed for ever, in that intense low register, to be without fun and games. With the baritones we are among pleasant fellows of this world, but I feel that with a little trouble I could do it nearly as well myself. The great bass alone unfailingly brings delight. (In Russia they have dozens of them.) This voice is magnificent and terrible and yet it belongs to us and is not lilting and trilling out of some other world. And this is how the joys and sorrows of Man should be celebrated, preferably with a full orchestra.

93

Blossom

Blossom – apple, pear, cherry, plum, almond blossom – in the sun. Up in the Dales when I was a child. In Picardy among the ruin of war. Afterwards at Cambridge and among the Chilterns, where I would read my publishers' manuscripts and review copies in their delicate shade. At the bottom of the canyons, at Bright Angel and Oak Creek, in Arizona. Here in our garden in the Isle of Wight. So many places, so much time; and yet after fifty years this delight in the foaming branches is unchanged. I believe that if I lived to be a thousand and were left with some glimmer of eyesight, this delight would remain. If only we could clean off the world from this Earth. But at least once every spring on a fine morning that is what we seem to do, as we stare again at the blossom and are back in Eden. We complain and complain, but we have lived and have seen the blossom – apple, pear, cherry, plum, almond blossom – in the sun; and the best among us cannot pretend they deserve – or could contrive – anything better.

94

Free passes

Being given free passes for theatres, exhibitions, sports grounds, railways, etc. The delight here does not spring from the thought that money has been saved. Indeed, I doubt if such a thought could ever bring genuine delight, except to a special miserly type. People are often quite ready to spend far more money, in various roundabout ways, to obtain one of these free passes than they could ever save by using it. No, the free pass is no mere money-saver. At its best, when it has a life of months or years and takes the shape of a metal badge or emblazoned card, the free pass seems to us a magical object, like some fairy gift. Not only does it admit us without payment but – and this is where the magic comes in – it lifts us at once high above the mob who must keep on paying. As owners of the free pass, we are special people, and may be seen, we feel, almost floating about with it. While the mob are struggling to produce their ten-bob notes or sticky half-crowns, we are murmuring *Open Sesame* and are being wafted inside. That, at least, is how we feel about it. But I must admit that with me the delight comes from receiving the free pass and not from actually making use of it. When one comes my way – and I have had various kinds in my time – I recognise it for the magical object it is, and I chuckle and crow, and for a day or two keep taking another look at it, still delighted. But ironically enough, once I have been given a free pass I rarely find any opportunity to use it. I remember being given a pass that entitled me to free first-class travel, for a whole year, anywhere between London and Aberdeen. Gloating over it, I saw myself departing from or alighting at King's Cross every other day or so; but it is a fact that during all those twelve months I made only one journey on that particular line. Again, having written an article praising a certain sport, I was given a card of admittance that was valid for years; but I never used it once. And for a long time, before the war, I had a free pass to one of our largest music halls; but I can never remember using it. What I do not forget, however, is my delight when these passes arrived – and indeed, although this happy traffic is not what it was, when they still arrive. Then, with the badge or card in my hand, I join Wordsworth as he lies on the grass and listens to the cuckoo, for to both of us magic has come and this earth "Again appears to be an unsubstantial færy place...."

95

Making stew

Making stew. It is not often I am allowed to do this; and indeed my great stew-making time was during the darker hours of the war, when anything was about to happen. But I am always delighted to make stew. And it is unusually good stew. You might travel from Truro to Inverness, even today, and be offered nothing better than or as good as my stew. One of my children, without any prompting from me, once ate four large helpings of it. My stew is thick, nourishing and wonderfully tasty. It has meat in it, but almost any kind of meat will do. I add all vegetables that are in season and in the house. And when I am in the mood I toss in exquisite little dumplings. After hours of simmering and thickening and thinning, for I never rush the business and keep peering into the pan, tasting, muttering a spell or two, I add any red wine that I can lay my hands on, and then, at the last moment, drop in a spoonful of honey. The stew is then ready. The very smell is princely. All men and all children gobble my stew gratefully. The women, who hate us to master their little arts, pretend to taste dubiously, arch their brows, wrinkle their noses, ask what is in it, complain about the mess in the kitchen; but nevertheless they contrive in a rather absent-minded manner to eat their share of the noble dish. How can they help it? Here is a stew that has been seasoned with many onions, red wine and honey – and my delight.

96

No school report

We fathers of families have one secret little source of delight that is closed to other men. As we read the school reports upon our children, we realise with a sense of relief that can rise to delight that – thank heaven – nobody is reporting in this fashion upon us. What a nightmare it would be if our personalities were put through this mincing machine! I can imagine my own report: *"Height and weight at beginning of term - 5 feet, 9 inches*: 13 *stone,* 10 *lbs. At end of term – 5 feet, 8 inches*: 14 *stone,* 2 *lbs.* Note: Through greed and lack of exercise, J. B. is putting on weight and is sagging. He must get out more and eat and drink less. *Conduct* – Not satisfactory. J. B. is increasingly irritable, inconsiderate, and unco-operative. He is inclined to blame others for faults in himself. He complains of lack of sleep but persists in remaining awake to finish rubbishy detective stories. He smokes far too much, and on several occasions has been discovered smoking in bed. There is no real harm in him but at the present time he tends to be self-indulgent, lazy, vain and touchy. He should be encouraged to spend some weeks this summer with the Sea Scouts or at a Harvest Camp. *Eng. Lang. & Lit.*: Fair but inclined to be careless. *French*: A disappointing term. *History*: Has not made the progress here that we expected of him. Should read more. *Mathematics*: Very poor. *Art*: Has made some attempts both at oils and water-colour but shows little aptitude. Has been slack in his Appreciation and did not attend Miss Mulberry's excellent talks on the Italian Primitives. *Music*: Fair, but will not practise. *Natural History*: Still professes an interest but finds it impossible to remember names of birds, butterflies, flowers. Has not joined in the Rambles this term. *Chemistry*: Clearly has no interest in this subject. *Physics*: Poor, though occasionally shows interest. Fails to comprehend basic laws. *Physical Culture*: Sergeant Beefer reports that J. B. has been frequently absent and is obviously far from keen. A bad term. *General Report*: J. B. is not the bright and helpful member of our little community that he once promised to be. He lacks self-discipline and does not try to cultivate a cheery outlook. There are times when he still exerts himself – e.g. he made a useful contribution to the end of term production of *A Comedy of Errors* – but he tends to be lazy and egoistical. His housemaster has had a talk with him, but I suggest that stronger parental guidance would be helpful, and is indeed necessary." And then I would be asked to see my father, and would find him staring and frowning at this report, and then he would stare and frown at me and would begin asking me, in his deep and rather frightening voice, what on earth was the matter with me. But it can't happen, not this side of the grave. I am knee-deep in the soggy world of greying hair and rotting teeth, of monstrous taxes and overdrafts, of vanishing friends and fading sight; but at least, I can tell myself delightedly, nobody is writing a school report on me.

97

Seeing the North

Our souls have their own geographical loyalties, quite distinct from such tastes as we ourselves may have cultivated. There are, we will say, five regions: the North, above latitude 55; Southern English; Mediterranean; Desert; and Lush Tropical. Now I live, by choice, in the Southern English region. When I could manage it, I used to go for holidays to the Mediterranean or Desert regions, with occasional excursions into the Lush Tropics. I deeply appreciate our Southern English climate, landscape, flora, and, at a pinch, fauna. I admire the landscape and seascape of the Mediterranean region, with its classical air, its odd mixture of smiles and severity. The Desert draws me, and often I find myself hungering for another sight of it. The Lush Tropics I always greet with enthusiasm, but I am never at home in them, and very soon I become half-bored, half-frightened, as I do in wars. I do not like their sudden glares and huge green glooms, their impudent sweetness, their abysses of stinking decay. I do not belong down there. Give me, I say, the Desert or the Mediterranean or, better still for a long stay, our exquisitely temperate Southern England. But this is not what my soul says. It is when we cross latitude 55 and reach the North that my soul, quite without any prompting from me, cries out in delight. I remember such a cry when we had been travelling as far south as Tahiti and had seen all that is lushest on this earth, together with some American versions of the Desert and Mediterranean regions; and then had flown north, to find ourselves in British Columbia. And at the sight of the cold peaks there, the slopes of pine and fir, the streams that looked as if they came from springs of crème-de-menthe and Guinness, the infinitely hopeful green of the valleys, the pale hollow of the sky, it was not I, who have no particular taste or fancy for these things, but the soul within me that sent up a shout of delight. As if at last I had brought it home. But why, when I have never lived in such places nor choose to make holiday in them, my soul should behave like this is a mystery to me.

98

After a concert

After a good concert. First, no matter how good it has been, I am glad it is over and that I need no longer keep still and quiet but can move about, talk, laugh, smoke, and perhaps eat and drink. But the music has done something to me. I feel refreshed inside, loosened up and easy, no longer an angry dwarf but a careless smiling giant. The night looks better than it did when I hurried into the concert hall. It too is larger and looser, and holds more promise in its glitter and distances. I like the look of people, perhaps for the first time that day. Strangers seem pleasant acquaintances; acquaintances turn into friends; and friends now seem well-tried, old and dear. This is the hour, I feel, to give and receive confidences, confessions of the soul. Somehow the world outside the hall seems to reflect the noble patterns of sound. Still held aloft on the shoulders of Bach and Mozart, Beethoven and Brahms, I can take a longer view, a broader outlook, and can believe that the good life is not yet a lost dream. Ten minutes wait for a taxi – and the mood will be gone; but while it lasted and the green sap seemed to be rising in the Tree of Life – what delight!

99

Buying books

Buying books. I will admit that the delight here is only a shadow of what it once was. I have spent too long behind the scenes in the making of books. But when I was in my middle teens, trying to be a clerk in a wool office, buying books was my joy. I had very little money then, and in order to find the necessary shillings for the *Everyman* and *World's Classics* volumes that were my first choice, I had to discover some way of saving money on my lunches. There was a place in the covered-market where you could buy a bag of stale buns for tuppence. There were also the Health foods, which were cheap in those days. For about threepence you could buy two heavy little slabs of mashed nuts and dates, sometimes with a sandwich-filling of chocolate; and these may not have satisfied my young appetite but they did succeed in temporarily murdering it as with a blunt instrument. With the pennies I saved in this fashion I would buy the *Everyman* edition of the Longer Poems of Wordsworth or some such dreary monster as the *Kalevala*.

I rushed them home to my attic room, where I had converted several orange boxes, nicely trimmed and stained, into bookcases. The shelves and the books were light enough, but their literary culture weighed tons. My taste in those years – and quite right too – was for what our forefathers called the *Sublime*, usually in small type on the thinnest India paper. Sitting close to my angry little gas-fire, which could only begin to warm my hands by first roasting my feet, I would spend an hour or so with one of the world's giants, in all the hungry solemnity of a seventeen-year-old, and would then compose free verse, frequently on the subject of Atlantis. Having once gone half-empty to acquaint myself with the *Sublime*, now that I am fat and full I consider that I need not bother with it. But now and again, unwrapping a parcel, I notice a quiver of that old delight in acquiring books and filling yet another shelf. And the shilling masterpieces I bought so long ago are still with me. I have no difficulty in recognising them once I have peeped inside their covers, for in each of them is written "J. Boynton Priestley" (for so I described myself, to give myself age and weight and perhaps a touch of the *Sublime*): telling the world that this book, which had cost two helpings of steak pie and fig pudding, was mine. And perhaps when I am older, these may be the books I shall want, to begin my reading all over again, returning to the Hundred Best Books, getting bogged once more in the *Kalevala*.

100

View from my study

Possessing a wonderful view. But first - a word about this possession. It has an ugly ring. There is a *Keep Off the Grass* sound about it. "This is my view, not yours. Push off!" But in this narrow sense I do not own the view. If you take the trouble to come this way, then you can enjoy most of it too. I only possess it in the sense that it is always there for me if I want it. There is a double delight here for me, for achievement has been added to possession. All my life I have hankered after a study that would be high up, have a fine large window and a broad window seat, and would look out upon a glorious view. As some men climb politically or socially, so for years I have been climbing topographically and domestically. Each workroom I acquired was higher than the last. And now I am where I have always wanted to be, and do not expect to do better this side of the grave. So much for achievement.

But the view itself is very special. I might have put it together myself, like the scenery of our dreams. There is in this view nearly everything I love in the English scene. Down below on the right are downlands and heath, green slopes and gorse in bloom. Lower and nearer the centre are cultivated fields, then, toward the left, some woods, and beyond, just in the picture, a glimpse of a tiny church, some cottages, and the ruin of a large manor house. Further off, but dominating the scene, is the long chalk cliff that ends in the Needles, which have been to so many travellers the first sign of England. And full in the middle panes of my window is that flashing mirror, that blue diamond or that infinite haze, that window for the mind, which is the sea. I hold this tenure of the delighted eye in the most precarious world since the Ice Age. My security is as brittle as the teeth I am fast losing. But I have arrived at my high window; I have already lolled on the broad seat; I have looked down by the hour upon the gorse, the woods, the cliffs, the sea; and the glory my eyes have seen – praise the Lord! – cannot be robbed of its yesterdays. So, all you haters of our happiness – sucks to you!

101

Reading about the Pink 'Un set

Reading about the *Pink 'Un* set. This delight illustrates
the difference between literature and life. I dislike racing.
Nearly all the sporting gents I have met have irritated or
bored me. I detest late suppers, the musical comedy world,
and long funny stories. One meal at Romano's in its
prime, I imagine, would have been more than enough for
me. One night with Pitcher, Shifter, Swears and the rest,
would have been too much for me. Yet for years I have
delighted in reading about this boozy set and all their
raffish pals and lovely little ladies. Without regret I have
thrown away hours and hours, which might well have
been devoted to literature or the problems of the modern
world, running up to Newmarket or down to Brighton
with Mr. Binstead and his friends, popping into the Gaiety
or the Palace with them, calling for a magnum of "Boy"
and four dozen oysters, looking in at the Pelican to hear

another yarn or two about Bessie Bellwood or Fatty Coleman. These sagas of Fleet Street, the old Strand, Leicester Square and Epsom have taught me nothing except a short cut or two to the bankruptcy court, the hospital and the grave. They have wit and humour but it is the kind of wit and humour that shines much brighter after six double whiskies. The characters are over-rated. The anecdotes are too long. Their style, except for Binstead at his best, is horrible, with more than a hint of the auctioneer and estate agent in it. And to me there is nothing topical about them, for I was a small child when these chaps were roaring round the town. Yet I still find this gossip and nonsense strangely fascinating, as if this little lost sporting-and-dramatic world of the 'eighties and 'nineties had once been my world. I can even discover a flicker of pathos in these chronicles. Is there somewhere among them a dim figure, a very minor character without a name, who once shared a cab with Pitcher or mince pie and brandy with Swears at the Pelican, who was myself in a previous incarnation, and who, after a fatal stroke in a chophouse or the Empire bar, was flung at once by the Wheel into existence again, this time among the Baptists in the West Riding?

102

Orchestras creeping in to piano

I do not care where it happens, whether it is at the Coketown Hippodrome or the Royal Albert Hall, or who brings it off, whether it is Billy Binks, the Comedy Entertainer, or Strugg, the World's Greatest Pianist, but I never fail to get into a dingle-dangle of delight, with icy-legged spiders racing up and down my spine, when suddenly and softly the orchestra creeps in to accompany the piano. You have not heard the orchestra for some time, only the piano. You have almost forgotten about orchestras. And suddenly – and oh so softly at first – there it is, with the strings whispering below the familiar silver hammering of the piano, then the wood wind bubbling and chuckling, then the brass assertive and triumphant, then the drums and cymbals booming and clashing to a grand finality. Socrates was wiser than I am; Alexander and Caesar made bigger names for themselves; and Shakespeare could write much better than I can. But not one of them ever heard the orchestra come creeping in to support the piano and never knew my dingle-dangle of delight.

103

Cooking picnics

Like most men and unlike nearly all women, those atavistic creatures, I detest picnics. One reason is that I am usually very hungry out in the open and I dislike the kind of food provided by picnics. Thus, there are few things to eat better than a properly dressed salad in a fine big salad bowl, but there are few things less appetising than an undressed salad out of a paper bag or cardboard box. Then, except for thick slices of ham between thin slices of bread, I have a growing distaste for the whole sandwich family, especially paste, egg or cheese sandwiches. Again, anything with jam in it or on it is a curse on a summer's day. Finally, there is a peculiarly hard, green, sour little apple that must be grown specially for picnic boxes. Nevertheless, I have delighted in my time – and am not yet past it – in one kind of picnic, namely, the cooking picnic. This is for great souls. The instrumental basis of it is the frying-pan. Sausages will do, though steak of course is better. Fried potatoes are essential, and persons whose stomachs shrink from a greasy chip rather underdone should stay at home and nibble health foods. Coffee, which stands up to wood smoke better than tea, is the beverage. The cooking picnic is, I will admit, a smoky job, at least in this damp climate of ours. I have superintended cooking picnics – and I am a natural superintendent on all these occasions – with inflamed and streaming eyes and every sinus wrecked, spluttering and coughing and choking, damning and blasting, glaring at would-be help-ful children until they ran away and howled. I have stoked and fried and stewed and dished out portions until there was nothing left for me but a few bits of greasy muck and half a cup of coffee grounds. And even my pipe has tasted all wrong in the inferno of wood smoke. Yet I would not have missed a moment of it for a five-pound lunch in a private room on somebody else's expense sheet. Somewhere among the damp obstinate sticks, the dwin-dling sausages, the vanishing fat, the potatoes that would not brown and the water that would not boil, the billow-ing smoke on the hillside, the monstrous appetites of the company, there has been delight like a crumb of gold.

104

Beginning to cast a play

Beginning to cast a play. No, this is not quite accurate. Strictly speaking, the delightful time is just before getting down to the actual business of casting. It is when three or four of you, all concerned in the play's production, cosily foregather to exchange airy talk about the possible cast. You all have your feet well off the ground. To protect the happy speculative mood, the door is bolted against brute facts. Other managements, the films, and all agents are forgotten. Here is the wonderful play, and here, eager to perform it, are innumerable brilliant players, all the golden lads and girls of the capital. How about So-and-so for the young man? Perfect! And Such-and-such for his father? Marvellous! How about Bracegirdle and Woffington, Garrick and Kean? Just what I was going to suggest! What a play, what a cast, what a production! And you have only to keep this happy delirium going for an hour or two, to persuade yourselves that you have been working and have earned a drink, lunch, dinner, supper. And tomorrow, you tell each other as you go out, you will get down to it and start ringing up a few people, not one of whom will be free to appear in your play. Perhaps it would be better if this tomorrow were put off for ever. Little that happens afterwards can be as good as this hour or so of life in a fairy tale.

105

Waking to smell bacon, etc.

Waking just in time to smell coffee and bacon and eggs. And how rarely it happens! If there should be coffee and bacon and eggs (not all your eggs, of course) to smell, then it is long odds against our waking – or at least against *my* waking – just in time to smell them. If we should happen to waken bang on breakfast, then it is probably fifty to one against there being bacon *and* eggs *and* coffee all hot and suitably odorous. We live in a world of fantastic events and staggering coincidences. The papers are full of them. After listening to an hour of our talk these days, Sinbad the Sailor would roll out in disgust, calling us a pack of liars. Few of us ask to be immersed day after day in all this far-fetchedness. Most of us could do with a smaller, plainer but more companionable world. We plan, we toil, we suffer – in the hope of what? A camel-load of idols' eyes? The title deeds of Radio City? The Empire of

Asia? A trip to the moon? No, no, no, no. Simply to wake just in time to smell coffee and bacon and eggs. And, again I cry, how rarely it happens! But when it does happen – then what a moment, what a morning, what delight!

106

Sketches of C. J. Holmes

I never met C. J. Holmes. He was not a great artist, perhaps not even a considerable one. Yet few painters of this or any other age have given me more lasting delight than Holmes. The reason is that he did successfully what I have always wanted to do, have tried to do, and have grotesquely failed to do. For what he did was to slap down on paper any bit of landscape that took his eye. The medium, did not matter – he would use pencil, ink, chalk, pastel, watercolour, and if necessary mix them all up – but what he saw and enjoyed, mostly on holiday, I imagine, he recorded with speed and precision, catching a moment and holding it for ever. Anything would do, Lake District mountains, Oxfordshire streams and willows, haystacks or factories (I have examples of all these and of other things too), but clearly he had to feel happy and excited about what he saw and then get the thing down on paper as soon as possible. And I would not exchange these sketches for whole academies of laborious studio work. I have been surrounded for years by specimens of this happy holiday art of his, and I never look at them properly (for often we look without truly seeing) without a lift of the spirit. "This is what I saw that morning and this is what I felt about it," he shouts from the wall; and I give him an answering nod and grin. When he left London with a bag full of pencils, inks, chalks, pastels, watercolours and paper, to mooch about and have some fun, he was already on his way towards lighting up the existence of somebody he never knew. If I could do the job myself, then down would come the Holmeses and up would go the Priestleys; but I can't – and I know because I have tried. But, thanks to his sharp eye and quick clever hand, he has made me share his experience, rented me for a few guineas many a morning's happiness. Is this art? I no longer know nor care (I took a postgraduate course on Æsthetics), but it is delight and good enough for me.

107

Memoranda self

Discovering one's younger and worthier self. After thirty years I have just been dipping into a volume that looks like a ledger but is labelled *Memoranda*. (Nowadays I would never dare to call my notes "memoranda".) It has even an Index – *Criticism – common mistake in*; *Imagination – whether re-creative*? *Music – æsthetic of*: that sort of thing. Blake, Coleridge, Hazlitt, Jonson, Nietzsche, Plato, Rousseau, Shakespeare, Sophocles are among those examined and discussed. These are not lecture notes, although I had just arrived in Cambridge when I began this volume, but my own original observations. And some of them seem to me very sound too, even though they are portentous, each note weighing at least fifty-six pounds. What a chap I was in those days! There I was, living mostly on bread and cheese and boiled eggs, wearing an army tunic that had been dyed, none too successfully, a sad blue, puffing away at my Cut Cavendish, burying my nose in this ledger every night to make my point about "Industrialism and the Platonic Idea of the State" or "Shakespeare's method of conceiving character"! Suppose that youngster marched in now, to transfix me with his hungry and challenging look! What would he think? Fat old fraud? On the evidence of these "memoranda", *his* faults are plain to me. He is too pompous. He is a bit of a prig. He cannot tell the difference between critical commonplaces and genuinely original thought. But not only do I like him, I delight in him - "Memoranda" and all.

108

Van Hoven

Among vanished delights must be numbered the variety act of van Hoven. If he were still performing, I would go to see him tomorrow. Indeed, his act would be infinitely more valuable now, simply as catharsis, than it was in his own easy-going time; and if he were alive today he would be worth a twenty-thousand-pound annual subsidy from the Central Office of Information. Van Hoven was an American who entered vaudeville as a straight conjurer and then, having achieved a few droll disasters in his performance, soon decided to create a comic conjuring act, which he played for years in the music halls here. He disdained funny make-up and appeared in ordinary evening clothes, a pleasant-looking, rather nervous fellow, surrounded by apparatus. He was generally assisted by three urchins, who, to support him in some trick as labyrinthine and regressive as a Kafka novel, a trick never to be completed in this world, held quantities of eggs and blocks of ice, over which they stared at him balefully. He had no obvious comic business, made no jokes. He was simply trying to entertain you with a few conjuring tricks, but was defeated, with mounting ignominy, by the untiring malice of things. Even when he first arrived, pink and smiling, you sensed that all was not well, that already he was hoping against hope. Very soon he was fighting against total despair. Trick after trick went wrong. The urchins had to be moved around, and blocks of ice exchanged for eggs. Mechanical illusions that had worked perfectly in the shop or at rehearsal now refused all co-operation with him. Not a trick came off. The neat figure who first entered was soon a glistening ruin. His smiles were the last flutter of flags on a sinking battleship. His voice became a hoarse despairing whisper, the croaking of a doomed man. He tore off the sopping rags that were once a dress collar and tie. The eggs fell like ripe plums; the blocks of ice began to melt; the stage was a shambles. The urchins, summoned so lightheartedly, were now like the Fates. Trying to think of something that might possibly work, he looked at us with glazing eyes. The cruel lights rayed down on him there, fixed in a nightmare. The orchestra, playing the rapid incidental music of all triumphant conjurers, contrived a final irony. And I used to laugh so uproariously that it hurt and I would lose sight of the stage in a sudden red haze. But even then I must have felt that this was something more than a wonderfully energetic piece of clowning. And I was wrong to say that the desperate van Hoven would be better than ever now. He might cut too deep, and we might all burst into tears. All he asked for was to entertain us with a few conjuring tricks, and look what happened. All most of us ask for now is a quiet life, and what do we get? Van Hoven has left us but now we are all in his world. Any newspaper will show us the tricks going wrong, the ice melting, the eggs falling....

109

Solemn antics of boyhood

The solemn antics of boyhood. There was, for instance, a certain Christmas Day, about forty-five years ago. Among my presents that morning were a football and a red-and-white striped football shirt. I put on the shirt and took the football out to the nearest field, which was, I distinctly remember, covered with snow. (We always had snow for Christmas when I was a boy.) It was a leaden morning, with the weight of a dozen sullen Sundays pressing upon it; but round and round that field I went, kicking my beautiful football, now dribbling along the wing past four or five imaginary opponents, now dashing in towards invisible posts and nets to score tremendous goals. I was as solitary as Robinson Crusoe, and quite happy, grandly conscious of myself in my red-and-white stripes. Then, in the afternoon, when parents and relatives, somnolent after the huge Christmas dinner of that time, were muttering and snoring and no use to a boy, I went to play with the boy next door. He had been given an angry little engine that worked a miniature minting press. All that it could print were two smudgy ducks, but they were good enough for my friend and me. After collecting every bit of waste-paper in the house, we spent hours keeping the engine going and printing hundreds and hundreds of ducks, smudgier and smudgier ducks. It was a day of pure delight, and I could not buy one like it now for a thousand pounds.

110

Departing guests

I am more of a host than a guest. I like people to stay with me but do not much care about staying with them, and usually say I am too busy. The only people we ask to stay with us are people we like – I do not believe in business hospitality, which has the seed of corruption in it – and all Friday I work in a pleasant glow just because I know some nice people are coming down by the last train. I am genuinely glad to see them. But I suspect that I am still more delighted when they go, and the house is ours again. It is not that I feel that I have been mistaken in these guests, though this has happened of course at times. After the week-end I may like them more than ever, having discovered new virtues and unsuspected charms. Nevertheless, I am delighted to see them go. They leave more room in which to live properly. Meals are quicker and easier. There is no more hanging about, no more sight-seeing, no further necessity for bright talk. My mind, like my body, puts on its old clothes again. I enjoy hard work (my own kind) and foolish play, and both are difficult when you are cluttered up with guests. I like to think about life in this world, and it is not easy to do this when animated and talkative pieces of it are all over the place. With guests about I am conscious of myself as a solid, but as soon as they have gone I expand into a gas again. And a gas can have more delight than a solid. So – *Goodbye!... Good-bye!... Good –*

111

Timeless mornings

There is one kind of morning in early summer that is for me very special, the most delightful of all mornings. The sun is up and blazing somewhere but not visible yet down here, where there is a lot of gold mist about and the birds are singing from lost thickets. The warmth has not yet broken through, and the air has a cool sparkle: it is as if we were on mountains, high mountains but far south. Distances are hidden but everything close is sharply defined, very clear and gay, like new celestial toys. The hour has immense promise; perhaps Doomsday has come and gone. But what makes this kind of morning very special, the most delightful of all, is that it has a unique trick of lifting me out of time: I seem to be moving along a fifth dimension and to have a four-dimensional outlook. Or put it more sensibly like this. These mornings link up directly and vividly with similar mornings in my past, so that I am aware of myself as I was then. Practising with the tug-of-war team at school. Coming out of that moorland hut – when was it? – about 1912. Camps and billets and trenches in the First World War. Walking early up the Backs at Cambridge. All these selves on similar mornings down the years. And freed from the brutal hurry of time, I see this life of mine as if it were a play by Tchehov, whose searching yet tender glance we seem to borrow at such moments. Everything matters, yet nothing matters. We have escaped from balance sheets, reports of progress. There are no itineraries, no goals. Success and failure are equally meaningless. Every detail is memorable, exquisite, catching at the heart; yet the totality is itself nothing but a long clear dream. Such is the timeless view; and it is on these mornings in early summer that I obtain a glimpse of it, and am shaken by delight.

112

Women and clothes

Women who say they are indifferent to clothes, like men who say they do not mind what they eat, should be distrusted: there is something wrong. And men who sneer at woman's passionate concern about dress should be banished to the woods. For my part I delight in women when they go into a conference-huddle over new clothes. They seem to me then most themselves and the furthest removed from my sex. They are at such times completely in their own world. They are half children, half witches. Note their attitude during these clothes conferences. For example, their absolutely clear-sighted realism about themselves. We chaps always peer at ourselves through a haze of goodwill. We never believe we are as fat or as thin and bony as other people say we are. The ladies are free of all such illusions. (Notice the direct level glances they give each other on these occasions.) So in their clothes conference, unlike all masculine conferences, there is no clash of illusions. All of them meet on the firm ground of fact. What is known is immediately taken into account: Kate's left shoulder is higher than her right; Meg is very broad across the hips; Phyllis has very short legs. The conference line – and very sensible too – is that we are all imperfect creatures, so how do we make the best of ourselves? (If politicians and their senior officials tried the same line at international conferences, they could change the world in a week.) Yet the whole clothes-huddle is not simply so much grim realism. There is one grand illusion that they all share and never dream of challenging. It is the belief that out of these clothes, with necessary swaps and alterations, beauty and witchery can emerge, that somewhere here is the beginning of an enchanted life. And I for one find this altogether delightful.

113

The delight that never was

The secret dream: the hunger that can never be fed. All my adult life I have been more or less a Socialist Intellectual. I have tried to make myself – and other people – aware of the harsh economic and industrial realities of our time. Again and again I have taken my notebooks and type-writer to the factories, the mines, the steel mills. I denounced or jeered at those colleagues who would not look. I wrote some of the first detailed accounts of the depressed areas. Having been brought up on the edge of it, I knew what life was like "back o' the mill". I did not discover the proletariat at Oxford or Cambridge, for the West Riding working-class was in my blood and bones. I grew up among Socialists. I watched the smoke thicken and the millionaires who made it ride away. I saw broken old women creep back to the mills, and young men wither because there was no work for them to do and nobody wanted them. I knew the saddest waste of all, the waste of human beings. If Socialism was the way out, then Socialism we must have. If it meant more and bigger factories, then we must have more and bigger factories. If it meant larger and larger cities, more and more bunga- lows, cinemas, football grounds, greyhound tracks, motor roads, personal appearances of film stars, boards and committees, hostels, organisations for the right use of leisure, clinics, identity cards, radio night and day in every home, press officers and propaganda, party bosses arrang- ing all our lives – very well, we had to have them. At the worst they were still better than the grey misery I had seen, the deep cancer of injustice. But there was never anything here for my own secret delight. Nothing for the hunger of the heart. Perhaps, for all my pretence of being up to the minute, I was not even living in the right age; and when I looked for my own enduring delight, I became an anachronism. When I caught myself off guard, last thing at night after too long a day, huddled in a train and too tired to read, coming out of a dress rehearsal into a wet Sunday midnight in Manchester or Sheffield, I would remember what I wanted, and it was always something quite different from what we were all demanding. Sometimes it seemed as if the capital of a tiny German dukedom, round about 1830, were nearer to my desire than anything my friends were planning or that I could help to bring into this world. I wanted a place with the dignity and style of a city, but reasonably small and clean, with genuine country only half an hour's walk from its centre, its single but superb theatre, its opera house, its symphony orchestra, its good restaurant always filled with friends. One little civilised place full of persons, with no nameless mob, no huge machinery of publicity, no glaring metropolis. To be myself in this one dear place, with a position as comfortable as an old slipper in a tiny sensible society; and not a caricature of myself in several continents. To come out of a late rehearsal and smell the lilac. To have a play done as well as it could be done, by tried colleagues, by friends, in the one familiar theatre; and not indifferently produced in a hundred different theatres, for large sums of money hastily removed from me by accountants and tax collectors. Not to be caught up and lost in the machinery of existence – as most of us are now – but to live simply and directly, like an artist, a philosopher, and in such a way that feeling, thought, action, were always closely allied, and last year's inspiration would be this year's achievement. No rushing about, no long-distance telephone calls, no expensive mountebanking, no losing touch with friends and admired colleagues, no running a career as if it were a damned great factory. Everything small but of fine quality, cosily within reach, and means and ends in sight of each other.

The delight that never was

Poky and provincial? Why, almost all the world's best work has been done in these conditions. Think of Athens, Florence, Elizabethan London, Weimar. And what has come out of Megapolis but rubbish and hysteria? But if I should be told – and my candid friends will be on to it before you can say *knife* – that now there never can be such a place outside a daydream left over from adolescence, then I can only nod and look away. But perhaps something like it, at least more like it than what we - no, no, I see. Fall in, comrades! Quick march! But one of us, as we go, still hugs the notion of something quite different, the delight that never was, on sea or land.

114

But this is where we came in

When we come to die, Dear Reader, we shall either fall asleep for ever or leave this life for some other existence. Now for many a year one of the best pleasures of the day for me has been its last, this drifting away from consciousness, sinking into sleep; all the more welcome to me because often I do not fall asleep easily. Again, I have always been delighted at the prospect of a new day, a fresh try, one more start, with perhaps a bit of magic waiting somewhere behind the morning. And as I am not good enough for heaven nor bad enough for hell, the territory and company in between ought not to be too disturbingly unfamiliar. So either way it ought to be all right, and there is no reason why I should be afraid. And indeed, though often timid as a hare, shrinking from dogs, horses, rough bathing, doubtful aircraft, I do not think I am much afraid of Death. But of course that black velvet curtain of his has to be hanging at the end of the corridor, so that every gleam of delight along there is easier to see. For instance – Fountains. I doubt if I ever saw one, even the smallest, without some tingling of – *But this is where we came in!*

The End